A Guide to Tracing the History of a Business

THE BUSINESS ARCHIVES COUNCIL
185 Tower Bridge Road
London SE1 2UF
Tel: 01 407 6110

THE BUSINESS ARCHIVES COUNCIL

A Guide to Tracing the History of a Business

John Orbell

Gower

Aldershot · Brookfield USA · Hong Kong · Singapore · Sydney

Published by
Gower Publishing Company Limited
Gower House
Croft Road
Aldershot
Hants GU11 3HR
England

Gower Publishing Company
Old Post Road
Brookfield
Vermont 05036
USA

338·7

British Library Cataloguing in Publication Data

Orbell, John
    A guide to tracing the history of a business.
    1. Business enterprises — Great Britain — History — Information services
    2. Business enterprise — Great Britain — History — Bibliography
    I. Title.
    338.7'07041   HC253

Library of Congress Cataloging-in-Publication Data

Orbell, John.
    A guide to tracing the history of a business.

    Bibliography: p.
    1. Business enterprises — History — Handbooks, manuals, etc. 2. Business enterprises — Historiography. 3. Business enterprises — Great Britain — History — Handbooks, manuals, etc. 4. Business enterprises — Great Britain — Historiography. I. Title.
    HD2321.07   1987   338.7'072   87-15505

ISBN 0 566 05591 0

Printed and bound in Great Britain by
Biddles Ltd, Guildford and King's Lynn

Contents

PART THREE
INFORMATION SOURCES OUTSIDE THE RECORDS OF
THE BUSINESS

Acknowledgements

I am extremely grateful to the following for their most helpful comments, corrections and additions to this book: Dr Chris Kitching and Dr Eileen Scarff of the Royal Commission on Historical Manuscripts; Dr John Post, Chris Cooper and other members of the staff of the Public Record Office; Phyll Melling and Stephen Freeth of Guildhall Library; and my fellow members of the Business Archives Council's Executive Committee – Edwin Green (Deputy Chairman), John Armstrong, Dr Edgar Jones, Michael Moss, Dr Phil Ollerenshaw, Lesley Richmond, Richard Storey and Alison Turton. Sam Twining, the Council's Chairman, has been one of the project's staunchest supporters and I am very grateful to him. Jean Clark typed and retyped the manuscript. Only she and I know how grateful I must be to her. Blame for any shortcomings which survive must by laid at my door.

John Orbell

Introduction

Few organisations are as well placed as the Business Archives Council to realise the burgeoning interest in the history of business. The Council receives numerous requests for advice on how to locate historical information about a given business. Many requests come from academic historians concerned with business history, but most come from other groups: family historians and genealogists; historians in other fields of study, for example art, architecture, agriculture, design, transport, technology, labour and politics; and from business organisations who are engaged in writing their history or, more commonly, who require information for their mainstream business activities.

In responding to this demand the Council has sponsored this guide which aims to outline in general terms the principal sources available for shedding light on the history of a business. It is not concerned with describing specific collections of records, nor with explaining the types of record available in a typical business archive. It does not provide answers to specific questions. Its function is to outline the breadth of source material available for researching the history of a business, to provide ideas and contacts, and to indicate further reading. *Above all it is designed as much for the enthusiast historian using business history sources as it is for the academic historian.*

Source material includes records created by the business itself but also a much wider and highly diverse group of materials not created by the business in which the researcher is interested. These include, for example, information held in the archives of the business's bankers or solicitors, information which it passed to different government agencies, and the reports on it which appeared in the press. The second section of this guide describes how to locate records created by the business and it covers reference books and organisations which provide advice and maintain registers. The third, more extensive, section describes other sources of information.

Half the battle in locating information about a business is won by discovering what actually happened to the business: is it still active?; is it dormant or defunct?; is it trading under a different name? Answers to these questions can lead directly to a business's archives. The first section of this Guide considers the procedure to adopt in order to locate the business if it is still active, or, if not, how to discover its fate. This section also outlines a strategy to adopt in undertaking research.

The addresses of all record offices, museums, libraries, societies and other organisations quoted are provided at the end of the text. Full bibliographical references to published works are provided in the text but are brought together in a comprehensive bibliography.

PART ONE

LOCATING THE BUSINESS AND RESEARCH STRATEGY

Sources for Locating the Business

The first and most obvious step in tracing information about a business is to discover if it is still active. No single reference book lists every active business in Britain but several standard reference books, when used together, provide reasonably comprehensive coverage for all but the smallest local companies. Telephone directories are an obvious, yet frequently overlooked, starting point while the following standard books, available in reference libraries, will be particularly helpful:

Who Owns Whom. United Kingdom and Republic of Ireland. This has been published annually since 1958 and lists the names of subsidiary companies together with the name and address of their parent. Many dormant subsidiaries – not listed in other reference books – are included.

Key British Enterprises. The Top 20,000 British Companies. This annual publication is arranged by name of company and is indexed by activity and geographical area. Address, date of establishment, sales figures, number of employees, and so on, are given.

Stock Exchange Official Year Book. This annual publication traces its origins to 1876 when it was known as the *Stock Exchange Year Book.* Its name changed to the above in 1934 when it incorporated *The Stock Exchange Official Intelligence.* The latter was first published in 1882 and, from then until 1898, was known as *Burdett's Official Intelligence.* The contents of these publications are limited to publicly quoted companies, but a good deal of basic information is provided, including address, function, date of formation and capital history for each company included. It should be used in conjunction with the *Stock Exchange Register of*

Defunct Companies (qv) which lists defunct publicly quoted companies which, presumably, would have appeared in these publications.

Kompass Directory. This annual publication carries much the same information as *Key British Enterprises*, but some companies are included which do not appear in the latter, and vice versa.

Britain's Top 2000 Private Companies and *Britain's Privately Owned Companies. Second 2000*. These annual publications provide name, address, directors' names and controlling companies, as well as certain trading and financial information.

Kelly's Manufacturers and Merchants Directory. This annual publication carries very basic details – largely name, address and function – of a very extensive number of businesses. Its coverage is much wider than any of the books mentioned above but several small local businesses are excluded.

Macmillan's Unquoted Companies. This annual publication provides financial and market profiles of 10,000 unquoted British companies. As such, it includes not just private companies but the principal subsidiaries of quoted companies. Address, activity, directors' names, registered number and financial, sales and other data are provided.

In addition there are a number of printed local (not national) directories covering businesses in cities or large towns together with directories covering specific industrial or commercial sectors. There is a section on directories as a source of historical information on pages 72 to 76. *Current British Directories* (10th edition 1985, first published 1953) is a useful guide to the directories published over the past three decades.

If no reference exists in these books the inference is that the company is either defunct, or has changed its name, or trades on a very small scale. *The Stock Exchange Register of Defunct Companies*, published periodically until 1980, is the only reference book which lists defunct businesses but its contents are restricted to that minority of companies (albeit over 23,000 in 1980) which have been publicly quoted. The contents are cumulative so that the 1980 volume contains details of all the entries which appeared in earlier volumes. Since 1980 annual supplements to the *Register* have appeared in the *Stock Exchange Official Year Book*.

In the absence of printed sources listing other defunct businesses or businesses which have changed their name or, indeed, small companies not covered by the above reference books, indexes held by the Registers of Companies in London (for companies registered in England and Wales), Edinburgh (for Scottish companies) and Belfast (for Northern Ireland companies since 1922) are indispensable. Each year registered companies (as a general rule identified by Ltd or plc appearing after their name) are obliged to supply the Registers with specific information which includes the company's 'registered' address. Currently around one million companies are on the Registers while about a further million companies, formerly on the Registers, are defunct.

For many years the Register of Companies for England and Wales, by far the largest Register, maintained a card index of currently registered companies. This is now held on microfiche and copies of it are supplied to reference and business libraries on a subscription basis. Alternatively it can be consulted in the Search Rooms of the Registers. It provides the name of the company and its registration number, the latter being the reference required in order to obtain the file kept on the company. This number is unique to the company and is not reallocated if the company becomes defunct. Since the mid-1970s most of the returns made by a company are held on microfiche which can be obtained from the Register at a cost (in 1986) of £1.00.

The Register for England and Wales also maintains indexes of changes in name and of defunct companies. The former index is now held in microfiche form for name changes since 1976 while the latter index has been held on microfiche since 1963. These, too, can be purchased on a subscription basis and are therefore available in good reference libraries. For the periods prior to 1976 and 1963 card indexes, available only in the London Search Room at Companies House, 65–71 City Road, London EC1Y 1BB, must be consulted.

These two indexes are indispensable for discovering the fate of a business but, apart from providing details of name changes and approximate date of dissolution, like the index of active companies they only give the company's registration number. This is needed to obtain the company's file although most files of dissolved companies have been destroyed. These files are considered in Part Three. Broadly similar records are maintained by the Registers in Edinburgh and Belfast for Scottish and Northern Irish companies (although some companies based in England are registered in Edinburgh and Belfast, and vice versa).

Basic details of registered companies have been published at or about the date of registration. The City Business Library holds a strip index of company names which provide registration details of English and Welsh (not Scottish or Irish) companies for the period 1856 to 1973. Where appropriate, there are details of appointment of liquidators for the period 1945 to 1973. This strip index also provides the key to locating details of registration as published in Parliamentary Papers (1856–1900), *Investors Guardian* (1901–1962) and Jordan's *Daily Register* (1962–1973). Copies of these publications are also available at the City Business Library, and they are described in more detail on pages 47 to 48. The strip index also provides the key to locating details of liquidated companies as published in *Stubbs' Gazette* (1945–1973). This publication is also held in the City Business Library. The strip index is supported by a card index giving details of company name changes and by a five volume alphabetical list of companies dissolved from 1856 to 1930.

The first joint stock companies (excluding those few formed in the late seventeenth and early eighteenth centuries and subsequently by Royal Charter) were authorised in the 1820s but the general establishment of companies was not permitted until 1844 when their formation was possible simply by providing certain information to the newly formed Register of Companies. However, most businesses ignored this new form of ownership and preferred to remain as partnerships or one man operations, even after the introduction of limited liability in the 1860s. Only around 1900 did registered companies become relatively numerous. Thus many businesses existing before the end of the nineteenth century do not appear in the records of the Registers and therefore discovering their fate is a much more difficult and hit-and-miss exercise. However, two sources are particularly helpful.

The first source is the official Gazettes, namely *The London Gazette* (first published as *The Oxford Gazette* in 1665) and *The Edinburgh Gazette* (first published in 1680). In the late eighteenth century *The London Gazette* was listing bankruptcies of partnerships and this grew to the extent that in 1785, 500 bankruptcies were listed, increasing to over 2000 per year by 1850. Of equal significance, after 1750 *The London Gazette* began to list dissolutions of partnerships. In 1785, 200 were noted rising to around 1500 per year by 1850. The Articles of Partnership, the 'constitution' of a partnership, stipulated the period for which a partnership would carry on business after which it would be dissolved and, if the partners agreed, reformed. Notices of dissolution often gave the name of this new partnership. The use of this most helpful source is facilitated by the existence of an annual index, often bound in with the Gazette, but which does *not* form part of the main index. The index exists for *The London Gazette* from 1785 until 1891 and for *The Edinburgh Gazette* from 1809. However, while bankruptcies were invariably reported, dissolutions were reported much less frequently. There was certainly no requirement to do so and thus this source is not comprehensive. Back runs of *The London Gazette* and *The Edinburgh Gazette*, especially for the eighteenth and nineteenth centuries, are not easily come by, but are available in some large reference and academic libraries. In addition to the *London* and *Edinburgh Gazettes*, *The Dublin Gazette*, known as *Iris Oifigiul* since 1922, covering Ireland (both South and North until 1922), was first published in 1705.

The second source is published directories. Directories listing businesses and notable individuals located in a specific city or county began to appear in the mid-eighteenth century. Then they related almost entirely to London but as the nineteenth century progressed so more areas were covered; directories became more comprehensive; and they were revised and republished at more frequent intervals. London, having the greatest concentration of both people and businesses, had directories published every year from before 1800. From the 1840s these are remarkably accurate and comprehensive and form an invaluable source for locating businesses in the capital.

Their usefulness in plotting the fate of a business is based on the assumption that dates of 'appearance' and 'disappearance' of the business's name in the directory represent dates of formation and dissolution. This will not always hold good as a business might move away from the area to which the directory relates, but

7

against this it should be noted that in the nineteenth century the 'mobility' of business was very limited. Directories are considered at greater length on pages 72 to 76.

The above directories are complemented by telephone directories which were first published, on a local basis, in the last two decades of the nineteenth century. In these early years subscribers were generally businesses. The survival rate of directories is very poor and their most probable location is city reference libraries. The Guildhall has copies for London published since 1881 and of some provincial directories for the years 1899 to 1903 and from 1941. The Telecom Technology Showcase has copies for London from 1880 and for the provinces from 1900, but its collection is only complete from 1920. The Showcase (in 1986) has very limited opening hours and seating capacity.

Research Strategy

Using one, or a combination, of the sources described above, changes in name, approximate years of operation and fate of the business can be determined, especially for businesses in existence after 1800. If the business remains active, its address will have been found, while if it is defunct at least an indication of year of disappearance will be known enabling further research to be more accurately focused. For some researchers the above information in itself might be sufficient to answer their questions but most will want more information.

If the company being researched still exists then it is obviously sensible to approach it for advice. It may be able to supply useful information by directing the researcher to a published history or a relevant magazine article; by providing a photocopy of a type-script history; by putting the researcher in touch with others who have investigated the company's history; by opening up its archives for research; or by advising the researcher where its archives are to be found if they have been deposited in a record office. However, if the company is to be approached the researcher should do basic background reading and bibliographical work beforehand to save wasting his/her and the company's time.

The researcher should question whether access to archives is actually required. Certainly the academic historian, seeking answers to complex questions by way of data analysis, will require access, but others with relatively simple demands may well find answers to their questions by using secondary sources as described in Part Three. If archives are used researchers should consult John Armstrong and Stephanie Jones *Business Documents. Their Origins, Sources and Use to the Historian* (London, 1987) which

9

describes and explains the main types of records created by a business. In approaching the business for assistance the guidelines provided on pages 12 to 13 may be helpful.

If the business is defunct then its records may have been destroyed. This will be especially so if the business disappeared many years ago. Before the 1940s business archives were not generally recognised as valuable historical documents and so no great effort was made to ensure their preservation. Largely since that date a network of publicly funded record offices has been established and they have very gradually acquired archives of both active and defunct businesses. Guides to record offices and to collections of business archives are considered in Part Two.

In certain circumstances archives of businesses wound up years ago will survive in the archives of other organisations. The best example is when a business is taken over and then wound up or loses its independent status. Its records might well become part of the records of the parent company. The clearing banks are an excellent example of this as their archives contain those of the hundreds of smaller banks which they absorbed during the nineteenth and early twentieth centuries.

Archives might also have survived amongst those of a management company, or in the archives of a company's solicitors, accountants, or liquidators, or with the courts. These possibilities are all considered in Part Three. Other records might have survived in the ownership of families which were closely associated with the business.

Before the paperwork explosion of recent years, the average small or medium sized business created only a tiny volume of records and the chances of their survival are consequently even less. Indeed, in the eighteenth century, certainly earlier and perhaps later, the costs of paper and writing materials, widespread illiteracy and innumeracy, and an unsophisticated and undemanding legal and administrative structure (except perhaps for dutiable goods) meant that many small businesses may have kept very few or even no records.

If no records survive, or if the surviving records are very incomplete, the researcher will have to rely heavily on secondary source material. It is truly amazing how much information can be discovered from this very wide range of materials. It includes printed materials such as annual reports, chairman's statements, newspaper reports, trade catalogues circulated by the business, trade directories, the trade press, and so on. It also includes the records of chambers of commerce, trade associations and various market organisations as well as the archives of those companies that provided services for the business, or which supplied it with capital goods or raw materials, or which purchased its output.

A word of warning should be given here. Many businesses, especially banks, solicitors and accountants, regard the records arising out of the services they provided to their customers as confidential. Access to 'recent' records will only be forthcoming with the customer's permission. *Some* of the issues involved are touched upon in R W Suddards 'The Lawyer and the Archivist Went Down to the Filing Room' *Archives*, 15, October 1981.

In conclusion it is worth reiterating that even where no archives of a business survive, a considerable amount of information can be gleaned from secondary sources. However, such information will often only be discovered by perseverance and imagination.

Approaching the Business

Having traced the business, and discovered that it is either active or the defunct 'subsidiary' of an active company, a careful approach to the company can be made in order to obtain its co-operation. A small number of business organisations have appointed archivists, on a full or part-time basis, to organise and administer access to their historical records and to respond to research enquiries generally. The Business Archives Council publishes a directory of its corporate members which maintain archive facilities under the title *Directory of Corporate Archives* (1985, revised ed 1987).

The majority of businesses have made no formal in-house provision for the care and administration of their historical records. Considerable goodwill is shown by many but some might regard making records available to outsiders as an unproductive task in that it diverts management resources from profit generating work. Other businesses might feel uneasy about making sensitive records available for research by outsiders. It follows that care should be taken in approaching a business and the following hints might prove useful:

a) Applications should be made in writing and indicate the reasons for seeking access and the questions to which answers are sought.

b) Requests to see a great deal of material (at least in the first instance) can cause a reluctance to co-operate simply because of a shortage of resources. Access is a privilege and not (in most cases) a right. An assertion of a 'right to see' often creates resistance.

c) The advantages of co-operation with the research being undertaken should be stressed to the business. Often the business can make productive use of the research undertaken by others in connection with its current business activity. Potential uses are outlined in John Orbell 'The Uses of Business Archives' *Record Aids* No 2 (Business Archives Council, 1984).

d) Co-operation is more likely if the researcher offers to show research results to the business for reading and comment prior to publication.

PART TWO

LOCATING RECORDS OF THE BUSINESS

Records Deposited in Record Offices

The business being studied might not have retained its old records in its offices under its direct control. There has been a substantial increase in the number of deposits of business records in record offices in recent years. Record offices are publicly funded institutions whose function is to accommodate, sort and catalogue records of historical interest, ensure their preservation, and make them available for research. They vary considerably in specialisation but no one office in Britain has specialised solely in collecting business records. Record offices fall into two broad categories.

LOCAL RECORD OFFICES

All county councils maintain a record office, while several cities and large towns do likewise – for example Birmingham, Chester, Coventry, Hull, and Portsmouth. The archives they collect are essentially of local interest and include not just those of business but of local authorities, schools, churches, charitable and professional associations, landowners, and notable individuals. Each office contains records of a wide range of businesses, although where an industry is geographically concentrated the holdings of the local record office will reflect this concentration. The most outstanding example is the Manuscripts Department of Guildhall Library in the City of London which holds extensive collections of archives of banks, insurance companies, discount houses, international trading companies and other businesses providing financial services. Lancashire Record Office, like other offices covering the coalfields, has useful collections of records of coal mining, while Tyne and Wear Archive Service has several valuable collections of shipbuilders' records. Extensive collections of records relating to shipping and the sea are to be found in Liverpool record offices.

Many local record offices publish annual reports which describe records deposited in the year being reviewed. A few have published general guides such as: F G Emmison *Guide to the Essex Record Office* (Chelmsford, 1969); R Sharpe France *Guide to the Lancashire Record Office* (Preston, 2nd ed 1962, revised ed 1985); A M Kennett *Archives and Records of the City of Chester* (Chester, 1985). Others have produced typescript hand lists, such as *Sources of Business and Industrial History in Leeds Archives Department* (1977). The Royal Commission on Historical Manuscripts compiles *Record Repositories in Great Britain. A Geographical Directory* (HMSO, 8th ed 1987).

SPECIALIST RECORD OFFICES

A number of museums and academic institutions have established record offices to house records relating to the areas in which they specialise, either as museums or as teaching and research institutions. The 'national' interest of such specialisations generally means that their collections are not local in character. Many have notable collections of business records. The National Maritime Museum collects records of shipping and shipbuilding companies and of companies and associations concerned with the sea such as marine insurance companies and Lloyd's Register of Shipping. The Museum also houses important classes of public records including many important papers from the Admiralty, the Royal Dockyards and the Registrar General of Shipping and Seamen. They are all well described in National Maritime Museum *Guide to the Manuscripts of the National Maritime Museum. Public Records, Business Records and Artificial Collections*, (Vol 2, London, 1980). The Science Museum houses several major collections, including records of locomotive builders. Glasgow

University Archives has extensive collections relating to business activity in the West of Scotland some of which are referred to in Peter Payne *Studies in Scottish Business History* (London, 1967) and in Michael Moss 'Forgotten Ledgers, Law and the Business Historian. Gleanings from the Adam Smith Business Records Collection' *Archives* 16 (October 1984). A guide is available on request. University College London has a major collection of records of British businesses connected with Latin America. The University of Reading's Institute of Agricultural History houses a major series of records of the agricultural support and food processing industries and of farming. It has published *Historical Farm Records. A Summary Guide to Manuscripts* (Reading, 1973). The University's Library is also a centre for records of publishing houses. The latter collection is described in J A Edwards 'Publishers' Archives at Reading University' *Business Archives*, 45, 1979. The Royal Air Force Museum has records of companies in the air transport and air frame building industries, while the Victoria and Albert Museum has records of businesses operating in the areas of art and design. The Modern Records Centre of the University of Warwick has an extensive collection of trades union records and a growing collection of employer associations' records, most notably those of The Confederation of British Industry and its predecessor bodies. These are well described in Richard Storey and Janet Druker *Guide to the Modern Records Centre* (Coventry, 1977), Richard Storey and Susan Edwards *Supplement to the Guide to the Modern Records Centre* (Coventry, 1981), and especially Richard Storey and Alistair Tough *Consolidated Guide to the Modern Records Centre* (Coventry, 1986). A further centre, though not strictly a record office, is the Institution of Electrical Engineers which has collected some business papers of electrical engineering companies. These are surveyed in Lenore Symons 'Archives and Records of the Institution of Electrical Engineers' *Archives*, 16, April 1983.

Details of specialist as well as local record offices, including addresses, telephone numbers and hours of opening, are available in Janet Foster and Julia Sheppard *British Archives. A Guide to Archive Resources in the United Kingdom* (London, 1982, revised 1984, 2nd edition in preparation 1987).

NATIONAL RECORD OFFICES

These are the Public Record Office (PRO), the Scottish Record Office (SRO) and the Public Record Office of Northern Ireland (PRONI). The first is concerned almost entirely with the records of central government departments, but the SRO and PRONI also house many private collections, often of national importance. PRONI, has, amongst a very extensive collection of business records, the records of Harland & Wolff plc, the shipbuilders, and of the Northern Bank. Some of the records held in the SRO are mentioned in J H Sime 'The Records of Engineering Firms and their Treatment in the Scottish Record Office' *Archives* 16, April 1983 and also in Peter Payne *Studies in Scottish Business History* (London, 1967). Records of several government departments, agencies and other institutions (see pages 42 to 57) contain a vast amount of information for the business historian. In this section it is sufficient to note that the PRO contains records of many individual businesses, although the records of several businesses were inadequately listed many years ago and are therefore difficult to access. These records, mostly found in series of legal papers (for example series J90 which is very well listed), were deposited with the Courts as evidence in legal actions, but never reclaimed.

Registers of Business Records

In discovering if a list of a business's records is available the following registers are of crucial importance.

NATIONAL REGISTER OF ARCHIVES (NRA)

The Register was established by the Royal Commission on Historical Manuscripts in 1945 to act as a central collecting point for information about manuscript sources for British history outside the public records. In the mid-1980s it is built around a series of about 30,000 unpublished reports on individual collections of records located mainly, but not exclusively, in Great Britain and Northern Ireland, together with published guides to record offices and surveys of particular kinds of records. Many of the reports are provided by record offices and libraries which have records in their care, but privately held papers are also strongly represented, including business records surveyed by the Business Archives Council, the Business Archives Council of Scotland and the Commission's own staff. The number of reports is growing at the rate of about 1000 per year. The Commission circulates copies of more important reports to the British Library; the Scottish Record Office and the National Library of Scotland, Edinburgh; the National Library of Wales, Aberystwyth; the Public Record Office of Northern Ireland, Belfast; the Bodleian Library, Oxford; Cambridge University Library; John Rylands University Library of Manchester; and the Institute of Historical Research, London. At the NRA there are a number of finding aids including a companies index arranged by business name and activity, and a personal names index (see page 83). The Commission's search room at Quality House, Quality Court, Chancery Lane, London WC2A 1HP is open to the public on weekdays (excluding public holidays) between 9.30am and 5.00pm. The Register answers specific written enquiries but is unable to respond to telephone enquiries. A series of publications is planned providing summaries of the more important lists of business archives held under the title *Sources for the History of British Business and Industry 1760-1914*. *Sources of Business History in the National Register of Archives* appeared annually from 1964 to 1972 giving very brief details of lists of business archives deposited. *Accessions to Repositories and Reports added to the National Register of Archives* is published annually, also by the Royal Commission on Historical Manuscripts.

NATIONAL REGISTER OF ARCHIVES (SCOTLAND) (NRAS)

This is based in the Scottish Record Office and in the mid-1980s holds around 2750 lists of records relating to Scotland. Some lists have been drawn up by the NRAS as a result of its surveys of records held by private owners including many business organisations. Others have been supplied by the Business Archives Council of Scotland and other record offices and libraries in Scotland. The Register's search room is at West Register House, Charlotte Square, Edinburgh, and is open from 9.00am to 4.45pm. NRAS reports are also filed in the NRA in London.

BUSINESS ARCHIVES COUNCIL (BAC)

Established in 1934, the Council (185 Tower Bridge Road, London SE1 2UF) has charitable status and draws its members from the business, archives and academic communities. Its objectives are to promote the preservation of business archives and the study of business history. In 1975, with support from the Royal Commission on Historical Manuscripts, it established a service to advise businesses on the organisation of their records, and to rescue valuable records in danger of destruction. Of more importance to the researcher seeking information about the archives of a business, the Council has undertaken a number of 'industry based' surveys which have located and listed records of historical interest. The industries covered include banking, insurance, shipping and shipbuilding and in all instances the results have been published (see pages 25 to 27). In addition, an extensive survey of the historical records of 1000 of the oldest registered companies has been completed. In undertaking work of this kind an information bank, covering the records of over five thousand businesses, has been built up. There is also a library of company history books. Visits to the Council's offices and library are by appointment only.

The Council's sister organisation, the Business Archives Council of Scotland, undertakes much surveying and rescuing work and maintains a publishing programme. Its lists are supplied to the NRAS.

Published Guides to Business Records

In recent years several guides have been published which describe the historical records of businesses belonging to specific industrial sectors, or based in specific geographical areas. These standard reference works are available in most good reference libraries. Also there are a few specialist journals, most notably *Business Archives*, which report on newly located records and on the content and uses of established collections of records.

JOURNALS AND OCCASIONAL PUBLICATIONS

Business Archives (*BA*)

This is the journal of the Business Archives Council. Since 1970 it has carried annual summaries of business records deposited in record offices. The summaries, which are classified by business activity, give the covering dates of the records, very brief details of the main classes of material involved, and the name of the record office where they are located. This information is based on the annual list of *Accessions to Repositories* prepared by the National Register of Archives and published by HMSO for the Historical Manuscripts Commission. In due course lists of most of the accessions recorded are filed in the National Register of Archives. *Business Archives* also contains articles on aspects of source material for business history. Examples of recent articles are: 'The Bryson Collection of Business Archives and Ephemera (in the specialist archive repository of National Museums and Galleries on Merseyside)' (*BA*, 47,1981), 'The Records of the Shipbuilders' and Repairers' National Association' (*BA*, 45, 1979), and 'The Uses of Registered Design Samples in the Public Record Office' (*BA*, 49, 1984). A number of articles describe the archives of specific businesses, for example The John Lewis Partnership (*BA*, 37, 1972), *The Times* (*BA*, 41, 1976), J Sainsbury Ltd (*BA*, 44, 1978), The House of Fraser Ltd (*BA*, 46, 1980) and Midland Bank plc (*BA*, 49, 1983).

Scottish Industrial History

This is the journal of the Business Archives Council of Scotland, and has been published since 1976 as the successor to the Council's *Newsletter* which first appeared in 1966. Its contents are broadly similar to those of *Business Archives* but much greater emphasis is placed on describing collections of business records.

MONOGRAPHS: BUSINESS SECTOR STUDIES

Banking

L S Pressnell and John Orbell *Guide to the Historical Records of British Banking* (Aldershot, 1985). This provides detailed descriptions of the surviving historical records of over 600 British banks. These include present day clearing banks, old London private banks, country banks established in the eighteenth and nineteenth centuries, joint stock banks which began to replace London private and country banks in the nineteenth century, merchant banks, British registered overseas banks, and discount companies. It also includes a useful summary history of the development of British banks and description of the main classes of records they hold. The book summarises the results of an extensive Business Archives Council survey financed by the banking community.

Insurance

H A L Cockerell and Edwin Green *The British Insurance Business 1547–1970* (London, 1976). This publication provides a summary of the results of a comprehensive survey of the historical records of the insurance industry, sponsored by the British Insurance Association between 1972 and 1975. It covers the records of about 275 active and defunct companies in the marine, fire, life and accident sectors of the business. Detailed results of the survey are deposited in the National Register of Archives.

Shipbuilding

L A Ritchie *Modern British Shipbuilding. A Guide to Historical Records* (London, 1980). This provides detailed descriptions of the historical records of about 110 shipbuilding and marine engineering companies in Britain, and in addition provides useful thumb nail histories of each concern. It carries the results of another Business Archives Council project which was sponsored by the Shipbuilders' and Repairers' National Association. In 1987 a second edition was in preparation.

Shipping

Peter Mathias and A W H Pearsall *Shipping. A Survey of Historical Records* (Newton Abbot, 1971). This describes, in very general terms, historical records in the possession of 35 shipping companies. There is a second section covering records deposited in record offices. However, as it was published in 1971, much of its information must be regarded as out of date.

Textiles

Patricia Hudson *The West Riding Wool Textile Industry. A Catalogue of Business Records from the Sixteenth to the Twentieth Century* (Edington, 1975). This provides very detailed descriptions of the historical records of about 125 textile concerns in the old administrative area of the West Riding of Yorkshire. The survey covers only records held in record offices and not those remaining with businesses.

Public Record Office of Northern Ireland (PRONI) *The Ulster Textile Industry. A Catalogue of Business Records in PRONI relating principally to the Linen Industry in Ulster* (Belfast, 1978). This provides detailed descriptions of records of textile merchants and manufacturers deposited in PRONI.

Coal

John Benson, Robert G Neville & Charles H Thompson *Bibliography of the British Coal Industry. Secondary Literature, Parliamentary and Departmental Papers, Mineral Maps and Plans, and a Guide to Sources* (Oxford, 1981). This publication considers a particularly wide range of research material, as its title indicates. The description of primary source material is arranged by location of records, rather than by name of company or colliery owner. British Coal's records are covered by a short entry as pre-nationalisation records have been deposited, some in the Public Record Office but most with local record offices and are described under these headings.

Registered Companies

Lesley Richmond and Bridget Stockford *Company Archives. A Survey of the Records of the First Registered Companies in England and Wales* (Aldershot, 1986). This highly important study summarises the results of a four year survey of the records of the earliest surviving companies on the London based Register of Companies for England and Wales, undertaken by the Business Archives Council (BAC). It describes the surviving records of 674 of these companies, and of their associated companies, and provides thumb nail histories of each concern. A great diversity of businesses is covered including iron and steel, engineering, transport, hotel, overseas trading, property, brewing, food processing and other manufacturing and service companies, together with professional associations, charitable organisations, educational institutions and political and sports clubs, all of which elected to vest their ownership in a limited company.

27

Altogether the records of over 1600 businesses are summarised, while full lists are deposited at the BAC and the National Register of Archives.

MONOGRAPHS: GEOGRAPHICAL STUDIES

British Dominions

Charles A Jones *Britain and the Dominions. A Guide to Business and Related Records in the United Kingdom Concerning Australia, Canada, New Zealand and South Africa* (Boston, Mass., 1978). This publication is arranged by location of records and not necessarily under the name of the company to which the records relate. It surveys in detail those historical records of a wide range of business organisations relating to their trading links with the Dominions. A greater emphasis is placed on describing records held in record offices but archives in the custody of businesses are covered.

Latin America

Peter Walne (ed) *A Guide to Manuscript Sources for the History of Latin America and the Caribbean in the British Isles* (Oxford, 1973). This contains a section on the records of a wide range of business organisations: banking and finance; contractors and consulting engineers; import and export houses; insurance, land, shipping, mining, milling, public utility and railway companies. Again, descriptions are restricted to those records covering links with Latin America.

Coventry

Joan Lane *Register of Business Records of Coventry and Related Areas* (Coventry, 1977). This provides a detailed description of the records of some 30 Coventry businesses, almost exclusively drawn from the mechanical engineering sector, especially motor vehicle

28

manufacture. There are useful thumb nail histories of each business. The survey claims to be the first attempt to catalogue records relating to the business history of a community. The publication can be purchased from the Modern Records Centre, University of Warwick.

Jane Lowe *A Guide to Sources in the History of the Cycle and Motor Industries in Coventry 1880-1939* (Coventry, 1982). This guide is in two sections. The first describes primary materials existing in record offices in Coventry and district and in the Public Record Office as well as with local organisations such as employers' associations and trade unions. The second section covers secondary materials, especially periodical articles and articles in the local press.

Australia, New Zealand and the Pacific

Phyllis Mander-Jones *Manuscripts in the British Isles relating to Australia, New Zealand and the Pacific* (Canberra, 1972). This volume describes those records in British archive collections which relate to Australia, New Zealand and the Pacific. Some businesses are included – virtually all London based – but only those sections of their archives relating to Australasia are described, often in great detail.

Far East, Middle East and Africa

Noel Matthews and M Doreen Wainwright *A Guide to Manuscripts and Documents in the British Isles Relating to the Far East* (Oxford, 1977); *A Guide to Manuscripts and Documents in the British Isles Relating to the Middle East and North Africa* (Oxford, 1980); *A Guide to Manuscripts and Documents in the British Isles Relating to Africa* (Oxford, 1971); and *A Guide to Western Manuscripts and Documents in the British Isles Relating to South and South East Asia* (Oxford, 1965).

Each volume contains some references to a few business records but once again just those parts of them relating to the countries under study.

29

North America

John W Raimo *A Guide to Manuscripts Relating to America in Great Britain and Ireland* (London, 1979). Once again some records held by businesses are described, together with relevant records held in record offices.

Canada

Valerie Bloomfield *Resources for Canadian Studies in Britain with some Reference to Europe* (2nd edition, 1983). This publication is along the same lines as that for America, described immediately above.

PART THREE

INFORMATION SOURCES OUTSIDE THE RECORDS OF THE BUSINESS

Records of Suppliers of Goods and Services

The records of suppliers of goods and services, and of customers can shed much light on the activities of a business. However, the records of those supplying services – banks, insurers, auditors, solicitors – tend to be the most useful simply because these businesses are easier to identify, often supplied services over many years, and have a tendency to keep their old records for long periods, relative to companies supplying goods.

SUPPLIERS OF GOODS

The extreme diversity of suppliers of goods to a given business precludes any comprehensive consideration of their records as a source of information. It is sufficient to offer examples. The records of civil engineers and contractors, which built factories, offices, shops, bridges, dams, roads, and so on, may shed light on a company's plant and major investment decisions. In studying the history of a shipping company, shipbuilders' records may be of major importance. Likewise records of locomotive builders and of iron and steel businesses making rails may help research on the history of railway companies. The records of the electrical and mechanical engineering industry, which supplied power plant, machine tools, etc, may help in researching businesses in a whole range of industries. For textile printing companies, the records of cotton and woollen cloth manufacturers may be useful, while the records of textile printers may shed light on the activities of clothing manufacturers. The records of suppliers of raw materials

– coal, oil, ores, metals, chemicals – might be of use in studying a very wide range of businesses, but in such cases suppliers are difficult to identify and are often large in number for any one business. The records of electricity generating and gas producing companies, if they survive in such detail, might provide useful information about a company's energy consumption and, therefore, output. Details of transport services, whether rail, sea, canal or road, might provide details of customer distribution and market. The reader will think of innumerable other examples, but the difficulties of identifying suppliers, especially of non-capital goods, are obvious.

BANKS

Banks provide a wide range of services for businesses. At one level they carry on the routine business of making and collecting payments for a business. At another level they make loans for medium term finance, and provide overdrafts and accept bills of exchange for short term finance. For long term finance they issue shares, debentures and other certificates of debt, and provide general corporate advice. Their records are of great use in shedding light on the businesses of their customers.

Historically six types of British banks are identifiable. Present day clearing banks were formed by amalgamation of a very large number of small banks – London private banks, country banks, and joint stock banks. With the exceptions of Coutts and Hoares, London private banks have ceased to exist or have lost their separate identity. They were first established in the seventeenth century, when West End banks tended to cater for private customers while City banks dealt with businesses. From the eighteenth century country banks began to be established in provincial towns and large villages while joint stock banks, with their multi-branch network, were an increasingly important feature of English banking from the 1820s. Such banks had existed in Scotland since the eighteenth century. In addition British-owned overseas banks, based in London but with branches abroad, provided banking services for businesses and individuals either located abroad or trading internationally. Most of these were formed from the mid-nineteenth century onwards. From the eighteenth century, merchant banks provided trade finance for merchants and later manufacturers, either based at home and trading internationally, or based abroad. Long term finance, through share and bond issues was also provided for British companies from the late nineteenth century onwards. The Bank of England, throughout its history, has functioned as a commercial bank and has provided facilities for businesses in the same way as other types of banks. Between the wars the Bank developed the important function of encouraging rationalisation of industries, especially old established staples, and the records it created then shed light on the activities of specific businesses and industrial sectors.

The records of banks are very diverse but major series include current and deposit ledgers giving details of transactions for account of customers; interview, character and other 'information' books giving details of facilities provided and of customer assets; minutes giving details of large loans requiring the sanction of committees; security registers giving details of assets pledged as backing for loans; and central filing registries, sometimes formed in the early twentieth century, containing files on major business clients and the facilities with which they were provided.

The British banking community has largely centralised its archives in head offices in London and Edinburgh where, in many cases, they are in the care of full time archivists. For lists and other information about banking records L S Pressnell and John Orbell *A Guide to the Historical Records of British Banking* (Aldershot, 1985) should be consulted.

Details of bank mergers, liquidations, name changes, location, and dates of establishment are contained in the annual *Bankers' Almanac and Year Book* (Thomas Skinner Directories), G L Grant *The Standard Catalogue of Provincial Banks and Bank Notes* (London, 1977) and James Douglas *Scottish Banknotes* (London , 1975). The latter gives short histories of past and present Scottish banks while F G Hilton Price *A Handbook of London Bankers* (London, 1890–91) gives a list of London banks (excluding merchant banks) for each year from 1670 to 1891. It also provides rather capricious histories of each bank, some of which extend to several pages but most to just a few lines.

Before the late nineteenth century many businesses raised long term finance by mortgaging their fixed assets and did not have recourse to bank overdrafts and short and medium term advances. When a property was mortgaged a mortgage deed was drawn up and invariably kept with the other deeds relating to the property. Large quantities of deeds are held in local record offices, often deposited by landowning families and firms of solicitors. Other deeds are held in large quantities in the Court of Chancery series in the Public Record Office. Useful introductions to deeds are N W Alcock *Old Title Deeds. A Guide for Local and Family Historians* (Chichester, 1986), A A Dibben *Title Deeds* (Historical Association, 1968) and J Cornwall *How to Read Old Title Deeds* (London, 1964).

INSURANCE COMPANIES

Business organisations were early users of fire, marine and accident insurance and in the nineteenth century their employees benefited increasingly from life insurance. Records of insurance companies are therefore of great use in seeking details of assets and employees.

All forms of insurance trace their origins far into history but fire, marine and life insurance began to take their modern form in the eighteenth century. Accident insurance did so a century later. Initially the insurance business was dominated by individual underwriters and by underwriting associations with a few major chartered companies or associations of partners appearing in the eighteenth century: the Sun Insurance Office, Royal Exchange Assurance, the London Assurance and the Phoenix. The formation of joint stock insurance companies began in the 1820s, a feature of this development being companies specialising in a particular geographical area or class of risk: plate glass; boilers, engines and mechanical plant; livestock; theatres; fine art; travel; and so on. In addition to insurance companies there existed organisations concerned with arranging underwriting of risks. The most notable was and is Lloyd's of London but there were also important bodies at Glasgow and Liverpool, for example the Glasgow Marine

Underwriters Association (whose archives are at Glasgow University). *The Insurance Directory and Year Book* (first published 1842) lists amalgamated, allied and wound up companies and gives appropriate dates.

Insurance companies record in detail the risks insured and their policy and claims registers are perhaps the most valuable of their records for information about a given business. Fire policy registers often contain name, address and occupation of the insured; their location; the type of construction and valuation of buildings, machinery, ships, etc; valuation and type of stock in trade; and so on. Buildings covered include textile mills, breweries, farm buildings, warehouses, potteries, sugar refineries, shops, paper mills, maltings, distilleries, and so on. Fortunately many old policy registers of the great London fire insurance companies have survived, most of which are located in Guildhall Library. They include 150 volumes of policy registers of the Hand-in-Hand Fire and Life Insurance Society covering the years 1690–*c*1820, 1260 volumes of Sun Insurance Office policies for 1710 to 1863, and 173 volumes of Royal Exchange Assurance policies for 1753 until *c*1830. The businesses of these companies were initially concentrated in London and the South East, but by the 1790s they were generally spread across the country so by this date the registers provide good national coverage. The usefulness of fire policy and claim registers is much reduced by frequent lack of indexes which causes considerable difficulties in tracing policies for a given business although there is a tendency for the policies sent in by a country agent to be grouped together making searches that little bit easier. Also, registers of many local agents of these companies survive, often in local record offices, and provide good regional coverage. Being less bulky and much more geographically specific, even without indexes they are much easier to use. Searching for policies for a given business in the registers of the Sun and Royal Exchange for the years 1775 to 1787 has been facilitated by the recent compilation of indexes (name, location, trade and others) financed by an Economic and Social Research Council grant. Microfiche copies of the index and accompanying essay by D T Jenkins *Indexes of the Fire Insurance Policies of the Sun Fire Office and the Royal Exchange Assurance 1775-1787* have been circulated to 250 university and polytechnic libraries, and record offices. Guildhall Library also possesses a forty drawer card index to Sun policies for the years 1714 to 1731.

Policy registers of life companies give details of employees and of their working conditions, especially from the late nineteenth century when life insurance of salary, if not wage, earners became common. Underwriting organisations have useful risk and loss books.

From their earliest days fire insurance companies had plans of premises drawn up in order to calculate more effectively risk and estimate premiums. Some plans, most of which were for industrial plant, have survived but they are far from numerous. An exception, which illustrates the value placed on plans by the fire offices, are plans and drawings, together with surveyors' reports, of London wharfs and warehouses prepared for the London Wharf and Warehouse Committee of the Fire Offices Committee. These are held at Guildhall Library and extend to 54 volumes of plans made between 1863 and 1903 and 20 volumes of surveyors' reports from 1864 to 1906. In the late nineteenth and in the twentieth century fire offices frequently acquired their maps and plans from external sources, especially from the firm of Chas. E Goad Ltd (see page 82).

The standard guide to insurance records is H A L Cockerell and Edwin Green *The British Insurance Business 1547–1970* (London, 1976) which is backed by the results of detailed field work which are filed in the National Register of Archives and at the Business Archives Council. The latter gives good coverage to policy registers and other records of local insurance agents. Information held in policy registers at Guildhall Library is described in an essay by D T Jenkins called 'The Practice of Insurance Against Fire 1750-1840 and Historical Research' published in O M Westall *The Historian and the Business of Insurance* (Manchester, 1984) and also in S D Chapman 'Business History from Insurance Policy Registers' *Business Archives*, 32, June 1970. Several hundred insurance policies relating to businesses involved in the Devon cloth industry have been transcribed and published by the last author in *The Devon Cloth Industry in the Eighteenth Century. Sun Fire Office Inventories of Merchants' and Manufacturers' Property*, (Devon & Cornwall Records Society, New Series, 23, 1978).

Maurice Beresford's essay 'Building History from Fire Insurance Records' in *Urban History Yearbook* 1976 provides useful hints for the quick searching of policy registers.

SOLICITORS

There is a dearth of published information about the historical activities of solicitors so it is difficult to relate any precise account of their work. Most frequently they advise in drafting contracts (including prospectuses) and deeds, and provide legal opinions, while most obviously they offer advice in legal disputes. The range of activities is diverse: the drafting of articles of association, articles of partnership, property deeds, contracts with suppliers, customers, staff and agents, agreements for the raising of finance, and so on. Also solicitors advised clients on the investment of their funds. Frequently copies of these records, and relating papers, have been retained on solicitors' files, while original documents may have been deposited with them for safe custody.

Many records of country solicitors have been deposited in county record offices while the British Records Association has played a major role in arranging the deposit in local record offices of records of many London based practices. However, the major London solicitors, specialising in commercial law, have tended to retain their records under their direct control. For an account of the work of one such firm Judy Slinn *A History of Freshfields* (London, 1984) should be consulted. Details of defunct firms of solicitors can be discovered through consulting back copies of the *Law Society Gazette* or the *Law List*.

ACCOUNTANTS

The records of firms of accountants are useful because of their two major historic functions, preparation of audited accounts and the liquidation of the business in difficulties.

While specialist accountants were at work in the eighteenth century it was not until the 1840s that the accounting profession – at least in England – began to develop its modern functions. Most large firms of accountants can trace their antecedents to this decade. In 1844 legislation enabled the general formation of joint stock companies and introduced company registration and the requirement to lodge an audited balance sheet with the Register of Companies. Although these compulsory accounting provisions were repealed in 1856 and not reintroduced until 1900, they did not remove the advisability (for the confidence of shareholders and the avoidance of fraud) or the necessity (because of a lack of internal expertise) of having external auditors. Also in the 1840s legislation regulated the liquidation of companies and made the appointment of an independent accountant a virtual necessity, although as early as 1831 the Bankruptcy Act provided for the appointment of an 'official assignee' – often an accountant – to liquidate a business on behalf of creditors. The functions of accountants have been modified over the years and details of their precise function and evolution can be obtained from Edgar Jones *Accountancy and the British Economy 1840–1980. The Evolution of Ernst & Whinney* (London, 1981).

Through these functions the records of accountants might include files on the financial performance, accounting procedures, annual results and liquidation of companies. Copies of audited accounts and annual reports, no longer held by the company, might also have been retained by its accountants. Until they were barred from doing so in the 1940s (although the practice had been frowned upon since the early twentieth century), auditors could sit on the boards of their client companies and board papers and correspondence might also be located in their archives.

Notwithstanding the importance of their function and the undoubted richness of their records, few records of accountants have been deposited in record offices. This is true of virtually all the leading national firms so application to them is essential.

ARCHITECTS, BUILDERS AND CONSULTING AND CIVIL ENGINEERS

The records of businesses involved in the design and construction of factories, office buildings and other plant are useful in studying the history of large businesses. These records might include

40

tenders and contracts, photographs, ledgers which indicate the costs involved, and plans and drawings. A set of plans and drawings may also be held by the business customer but when it vacates its premises, plans will probably pass to the new owner or tenant.

The Construction History Society and the British Architectural Library (Royal Institute of British Architects) are sources of advice concerning records and other materials relating to building and architecture. The former publishes an annual journal, *Construction History*. Many archives held by the latter are described in Angela Mace *The Royal Institute of British Architects. A Guide to its Archive and History* (London, 1986) but this excludes its holdings of archives of individual architects and their businesses. Edgar Jones *Industrial Architecture in Britain 1750–1939* (London, 1985) provides details of the work of architects in industry. The Royal Commission on Historical Manuscripts published between 1969 and 1974 *Architectural History and the Fine and Applied Arts: Sources in the National Register of Archives*.

ADVERTISING AGENCIES

Some large companies appointed advertising agents as early as the nineteenth century, especially if they manufactured or sold consumer goods. Records of such companies can be helpful if only through providing illustrative material. The History of Advertising Trust has sponsored a survey of sources for advertising history and has collected together some archives of advertising agents. It has also sponsored T R Nevett *Advertising in Britain. A History* (London, 1982) which, as well as providing a useful account of how the advertising industry developed, contains an extensive bibliography but is a disappointing route to discovering primary source material. One of the most important deposited archives of an advertising agency is that of Charles Barker Group Ltd, held at Guildhall Library.

Records of Government Departments

The records of government departments and agencies contain a mass of information about businesses and their environment. For example, departments and agencies regulate, protect and encourage industry; provide services and an environment for the efficient running of industry; and purchase goods and services from industry. It would be a hopeless task in the present context to cover in detail even the most promising sources shedding light on individual businesses. Accordingly, what follows serves to describe classes of outstanding importance in giving details of a mass of individual businesses, and to describe guides to discover information about less productive classes of records.

These other classes are of great variety. They include, for example, the records of the Admiralty containing details of ship victualling in the eighteenth century and ship purchases in the present century; records of the coal industry which relate to British Coal, formerly the National Coal Board, and colliery companies at the time of nationalisation; the Ministry of Power files containing numerous references to electricity supply, oil, gas and mining companies; the records of the Ministry of Munitions which made large scale purchases from British industry during the First World War; those of the Ministry of Supply which was responsible for Army and Air Force supplies during the Second World War; and the classes of records of the Ministry of Transport relating to shipping, railways, harbours and road transport. Many of these records will provide details of the activities of individual businesses but many of the classes will contain information about government policies concerning business and about the business environment generally.

Virtually all the records of government departments in England and Wales are located in the Public Record Office (PRO) which has branches at Kew and at Chancery Lane in central London. The division of records between the two sites is described in the PRO's leaflet *Information for Readers*. Generally speaking, records at Kew are of present and defunct government departments, public offices, etc, and are described in volumes 2 and 3 of *Guide to the Contents of the Public Record Office* (London, 1963–68). Chancery Lane houses legal records, records of some departments with quasi-legal functions and records of the State Paper Office. The Scottish Record Office (SRO) in Edinburgh houses records of pre-union (1707) Scotland, the Scottish Office and of government agencies in Scotland while the Public Record Office of Northern Ireland (PRONI) holds government records created in Northern Ireland. A new guide to the SRO is in preparation. Meanwhile M Livingstone *Guide to the Public Records of Scotland* (1905), although greatly out of date, is still useful for the older historical records. Details of accessions each year are given in the *Annual Report of the Keeper of the Records of Scotland*. The 1963–68 *Guide to the Contents of the Public Record Office* has now been re-placed by a guide in microfiche form, although the latter, in some instances, refers readers to the former for detailed information. Generally speaking, the microfiche guide gives covering dates, number of items, and a brief description for each class of records.

The most useful guide to records of interest to business historians in the Public Record Office is Brenda Swann and Maureen Turnbull *Records of Interest to Social Scientists 1919–1939* (Public Record Office Handbook 14, London, 1971). The covering dates are a misnomer as records of much earlier date are covered. The PRO also produces a series of excellent leaflets describing specific classes of records or records covering specific areas of study. They include, for example, 'Designs and Trade Marks: Registers and Representation'; 'Registration of Companies and Businesses'; 'Royal Warrant Holders and Household Servants'; 'Coal and Coal Mining'; and 'Records of the Registrar General of Shipping and Seamen'. Two journal articles are useful: T Rath 'Business Records in the Public Record Office in the Age of the Industrial Revolution' *Business History*, July 1975, and Charles Harvey 'Business Records at the Public Record Office'

Business Archives, November 1986. Some wide ranging papers on PRO sources for business history are published by the PRO in *Public Records Relating to Commerce and Industry* (PRO, 1985).

REGISTERS OF COMPANIES

The means of supervising the affairs of business organisations, for the benefit of both investors and public alike, have long pre-occupied legislators. The results of this supervision are no where more clearly manifested than in the returns which companies are obliged to make for public inspection at the Registers of Companies.

The 1844 Joint Stock Companies Act enabled the formation of companies with 25 or more members (ie shareholders), whose shares were freely transferable, through registration with the newly formed Register of Joint Stock Companies. The 1856 Joint Stock Companies Act required existing companies to re-register, reduced the minimum number of persons who could form themselves into a company to seven, and established Registers in Edinburgh and Dublin (transferred to Belfast in 1923 although pre-1923 records of defunct companies remain in Dublin) as well as in London. Limited liability had been introduced in 1855. Numerous other Company Acts have followed, drastically extending and consolidating this early legislation.

The role of the Registers in regulating businesses is crucial. Their main functions today are to incorporate and dissolve companies, to examine and file documents required to be deposited by companies under the terms of the Companies Acts, and to make this information available for public inspection. The files of the Registers are therefore of great help in shedding light on a business, but their content and survival has varied greatly over the years.

Files created under the 1844 Act are likely to include the name, purpose and address of the business; the names of a company's promoters and solicitors; a prospectus; details of capital issued and allocation of shares; and balance sheets. Files created under the 1856 Act usually consist of the memorandum and articles of association containing details of a company's constitution, its reasons for formation, and its function; an agreement with vendors if the company was formed to take over another business as a going concern; statement of nominal share capital; location of registered office; a register of directors; annual returns containing details of share capital and debentures and shareholders; and, in the case of dissolved companies, documents concerning liquidation and dissolution.

Unfortunately the 1856 Act removed the requirement for companies to submit an annual balance sheet to the Register. 1907 legislation required that an audited statement, in the form of a balance sheet, should be annexed to the annual returns made to the Registers. This balance sheet can be a useful document, especially in the event of the non-survival of the company's ledgers, but in the early years figures are often very nominal. It had to contain 'a summary of [the Company's] capital, its liabilities, and its assets, giving such particulars as will disclose the general nature of such liabilities and assets, and how the values of fixed assets have been arrived at....'

Unfortunately private companies, which were defined for the first time by the 1907 Act, were relieved from this requirement. However, this legislation failed to stipulate that an up-to-date balance sheet had to be filed, an omission put right in 1929 when the information which had to be disclosed in the filed balance sheet was extended. The balance sheet and the directors' report presented at the Annual General Meeting now had to be filed with the Registers. The Companies Act of 1948 distinguished between exempt and non-exempt private companies. The latter – by far the most numerous – were now also obliged to make a return of accounts.

The files of active companies are retained in their entirety and can be consulted at the Registers of Companies. The files of companies on the Register of Companies for England and Wales – by far the largest register – are primarily in microfiche form. Files are presented to researchers in the form of microfiche copies of original paper documents (at a cost of £1.00 per file in 1986). The paper files are held at the Register's base in Cardiff, or at its outstation at Pontypool, and can be inspected there. The entire content of each file is not reproduced in microfiche as annual returns and accounts more than three years old at the time of initial filming (ie 1976–78) and details of changes in directors, secretaries and registered offices more than seven years old at the time of initial filming, were excluded. All later documents were filmed, including formation documents and subsequent changes to articles of association and capital.

The files of defunct companies are kept by the Registers of Companies until they are about 20 years old when they are transferred to the Public Record Office, the Scottish Record Office and the Public Record Office of Northern Ireland. The paper files of companies on the England and Wales Register, dissolved prior to 1976 but not yet twenty years old, are held at the Register's London offices while the paper files of post-1976 dissolved companies are at Cardiff.

The files of dissolved companies are located in the Public Record Office in classes BT 41 (for companies registered under the 1844 Act and under the 1856 Act but dissolved before 1860) and BT 31 (for companies dissolved after 1860); in the Scottish Record Office in class BT 2; and in the Public Record Office of Northern Ireland in class COM 40. Reference to class BT 31 is by company registration number. From 1890, when liquidators were first required to file liquidation accounts, until 1932, these accounts have been preserved separately in the Public Record Office in class BT 34. Thereafter they are in the main company file in BT 31.

In the Public Record Office files for all companies dissolved before 1907 have survived but have been stripped of certain classes of documents. Thereafter, the files of all dissolved *public* companies have been retained although stripped especially with regard to annual returns. It was agreed in 1950 that all annual returns were to be destroyed except for the first, last and every intermediate fifth year (reduced to tenth year' in 1960). The survival of the files of dissolved private companies – defined for the first time in 1907 – is tiny as the Public Record Office retained only a one per cent sample until 1960. Then it was decided that files of all non-exempt dissolved private companies would be retained although stripped. In practice this affected files of companies dissolved from 1940. The practice of retaining a one per cent sample of the files of exempt private companies was continued but reduced to half a per cent in 1977. Sheets from the classified index of files for dissolved exempt private companies were kept to give brief details of papers registered on the destroyed files. These include name, number, registered office address and nature of business. They are available in the PRO in Class BT 95. The practice adopted by the Scottish Record Office and the Public Record Office of Northern Ireland differs from that of the Public Record Office. In Scotland, for example, the files of all dissolved companies have been retained intact.

Liquidators' accounts of companies registered in London between 1856 and 1915 and which were dissolved between 1890 and 1933 are held in class BT 34. Accounts of companies dissolved after 1933 are in BT 31. No liquidation accounts had to be filed before 1890. Class C 26 contains almost 700 files of proceedings and accounts in winding-up actions for the period 1849 to 1910. See also page 57.

A more immediate source of information about early joint stock companies is Parliamentary Papers (see page 80). Each year from 1856 until 1900 an annual list of companies registered in that year was printed by order of Parliament and is contained in Parliamentary Papers under the title Returns Relating to Joint Stock Companies. The list covers companies registered in England and Wales, Scotland and Ireland and each list is indexed by name of company. Against each name of company is provided objects of the company; place of business; registration date; total number of shares taken by subscribers to the memorandum of association; nominal capital and the number of shares into which it is divided; the number of shares subscribed for; the number of shareholders; and so on. Parliamentary Papers are to be found only in major academic or reference libraries. A set of just the Returns is available in the City Business Library in the City of London.

Information in Parliamentary Papers has been extracted from the returns made to the Registers of Companies. Similar information was extracted and published in *The Investors' Guardian and Limited Liability Review* (subsequently *Investors' Guardian*), published between 1863 and c1962. In its early years this weekly publication provided details of recently registered companies giving against name of company: registration date; objects; names of directors and their shareholdings; size of capital; number of shares; and so on. This became progressively less detailed, especially after 1918. It includes details of companies registered in

47

England, Scotland and Ireland, and there are periodic indexes of company names. Copies are scarce but a continuous run from 1901 to 1962 is housed in the City Business Library in the City of London.

Useful literature which considers the content and reliability of the returns, especially accounts, made to the Registers are Edgar Jones *Accountancy and the British Economy 1840–1940. The Evolution of Ernst & Whinney* (London, 1981) and J R Edwards *Company Legislation and Changing Patterns of Disclosure in British Company Accounts 1900–1940* (The Institute of Chartered Accountants in England and Wales, London, 1981). Sheila Marriner 'Company Financial Statements as Source Material for Business Historians' *Business History*, July 1980, is also helpful and has a useful precis of the main provisions of the Company Acts affecting the content, format and presentation of financial statements. Another useful article, written from a quite different perspective, is Christopher T and Michael J Watts 'Company Records as a Source for the Family Historian' *Genealogists' Magazine*, June 1983. Peter L Payne *The Early Scottish Limited Companies 1856–1895* (Edinburgh, 1980) provides an analysis of the 9000 or so companies registered in Scotland before 1895. The PRO leaflet 'Registration of Companies and Businesses' is helpful.

REGISTER OF BUSINESS NAMES

Partnerships were not required to register details of their activities until 1916 when the Register of Business Names was established in response to the Government's wish to have more precise knowledge of business ownership and activities at a time of war. Each business – regardless of its ownership status – was obliged to register its trading name, the name of its proprietor, its address and its business function. The difficulties of enforcing registration resulted in returns not being made by many businesses. The Register was abolished in 1982 when a sample of its records was placed in the Public Record Office in class BT 253. The sample comprises registration documents for a selection of businesses registered in 1916–17, and every ten years from 1921 until 1981–82.

BANKRUPTCY RECORDS

Legislation to deal with bankruptcy dates back to the reign of Elizabeth I. For much of this time cases of bankruptcy were dealt with by the Commissioners of Bankruptcy and, from 1831, by the Court of Bankruptcy. Bankruptcy was not uncommon as about 87,000 cases are recorded between 1780 and 1842 alone.

The Public Record Office contains large quantities of bankruptcy records but they are far from comprehensive and relate, at least in detail, to a fraction of bankrupt businesses. They break down into three basic categories. Indexes and registers give brief yet basic information about a very large number of businesses which got into difficulties. The general docket books in classes B 4 and B 6 give name, address and occupation of many bankrupts from 1710 to 1770 and from 1797 to 1869. Details of petitioning creditors are also provided until 1770 and in some cases after 1832. The second category is records relating to judgements of the Lord Chancellor, Court of Bankruptcy and Court of Review and provides detailed information about a small proportion of bankruptcies. The third category is files of proceedings each relating to a specific bankruptcy. These are in classes B3 and B9. The former relates to 4,350 bankruptcies between 1780 and 1842, about five per cent of the total. Some files contain very limited information while, at the other extreme, several bulky files might relate to one bankruptcy. These files *might* contain details about the circumstances of bankruptcy, a balance sheet showing the assets of the bankrupt, and information about claimants and dividends paid.

Equivalent records to B 3 and B 9 are preserved in the Scottish Record Office and are described in a handout available on request. These are sequestration proceedings and usually contain details of an examination of the parties before the court, and information about assets and debts and dividends paid. A computer-based index to sequestration cases from 1839 to 1913 is held as an on-line database in Glasgow University Archives. It is referred to in an article by M S Moss & J R Hume 'Business Failure in Scotland 1839–1913: A Research Note'*Business History* 25 1983.

In 1883 the Bankruptcy Act transferred the administrative function formerly exercised by the Courts to the Bankruptcy Department of the Board of Trade. Of the four classes BT 39 and

BT 40 are potentially the most useful in providing details of specific businesses. BT 39 contains 96 registers of deeds of arrangement covering the years 1888 to 1918, arranged in alphabetical order by bankrupt's name. BT 40 contains 29 Registers of Bankruptcies in the London and County Courts between 1870 to 1886. However, the introduction of limited liability, which was assumed by a rapidly increasing number of new and old businesses towards the end of the nineteenth century, inevitably meant that bankruptcy records relate more and more to individuals. Other PRO classes contain papers relating to bankruptcy, especially Chancery classes. C 217, for example, includes files of the Commissions of Bankruptcy, with evidence produced before them.

The London Gazette and The Edinburgh Gazette (see pages 6–7) carried various notices relating to the different stages of bankruptcy proceedings and much of this information was extracted and published in a number of volumes. These include William Bailey List of Bankrupts (London, 1794) which covers the years 1772 to 1793 in three volumes. Subsequent years are covered by William Smith & Co A List of Bankrupts with their Dividends, Certificate, etc, from Jan 1 1780 to June 24 1806 Inclusive (London, 1806); George Elwick A Complete Register of All Bankrupts (London, 1843) covering the years December 1820 to April 1843; and The Bankrupts' Register (annually 1833–48). Perry's Gazette (first published in April 1828 as Perry's Bankrupt & Insolvent Weekly Gazette) also carried weekly lists of bankrupts etc and had an annual index. It ceased publication in 1964. Copies of The Bankrupts' Register (minus issues for 1839, 1842 and 1844), and William Smith & Co.'s and George Elwick's publications are available in the British Library. The latter also has a full file of Perry's Gazette as does the Guildhall with the exception of issues for the years 1828–32 and from 1943.

A most helpful guide to bankruptcy records in the Public Record Office is Sheila Marriner 'English Bankruptcy Records and Statistics Before 1850' Economic History Review 33 1980. A leaflet called 'A Guide to Scottish Sequestrations 1839–1913' by John McLintock is available from the Scottish Record Office.

PATENTS

A patent protects the right of an individual to benefit from the usefulness of his invention by preventing exploitation of it by others, without permission, for a given period. While patent law became more sophisticated in the mid-nineteenth century – when the Patent Office was established – patents were granted much earlier. The earliest recorded in the Science Reference Library (Holborn, London) is dated 1617. Over the years, but especially from the late nineteenth century, the number of patents filed annually grew substantially. Over 17,000 applications were received in 1884 alone rising to 33,000 in 1982.

The usefulness of patents is various. Such a large 'bank' of information can be very valuable when virtually no information about a given business exists elsewhere. Patents give details of name, address and occupation of patentee(s). Where more than one patentee is named, collaboration between two or more businesses might be revealed. However, the bulk of information is technical and, to the general researcher, is uninformative other than offering a broad indication of the technical awareness of the business.

Patent specifications are printed documents, typically three to four pages long. They describe the invention and often contain diagrams and other illustrations. In addition, abridgements, being shortened versions of specifications which describe the invention in a paragraph, were also printed. A complete set of both exists in the Science Reference Library. The best provincial reference libraries also have comprehensive sets. *Patent Holdings in British Public Libraries* (Sheffield City Libraries, 1973) is helpful in locating them. The Science Reference Library has good finding aids arranged by name of patentee and, in some cases, by industry. Chronological indexes are also available. Some of these have been published and Bennet Woodcroft *Alphabetical Index of Patentees of Inventions* (London, 1854, republished 1969), which is an index of patents granted between 1617 and 1852, is the most widely available.

It should be noted that patents could be lodged in the name of an individual as opposed to the name of the business with which he was connected as, say, a partner. Others could be registered by a patent agent.

The Patent Office was established in 1853 and shortly afterwards it arranged for the printing of specifications filed prior to its establishment. These specifications were based on information held in various Chancery classes in the Public Record Office. The practice of enrolling detailed specifications of inventions, for which patents were granted, developed from 1711 onwards. Enrolment of specifications was either in the Rolls Chapel Office (see class C 73), the Petty Bag Office (see class C 210) or the Enrolment Office (see class C 54). From 1849 until 1853 all specifications were enrolled at the Enrolment Office.

Infringements of patents often give rise to legal cases. Official reports of patent cases since 1884 have been published annually as *Reports of Patent Design and Trade Mark Cases.* Earlier cases are scattered in various law journals.

H Harding *Patent Office Centenary. A Story of 100 Years in the Life and Work of the Patent Office* (London, 1953, reprinted 1975) provides a useful guide to the work of The Patent Office. Brian Winship 'Patents as an Historical Source' *Industrial Archaeology,* 1981 is a guide to using patents and finding aids relating to them.

REGISTERS AND REPRESENTATIONS OF DESIGNS

Since 1787 the law has offered a measure of protection for the exploitation of original designs, initially relating to textiles. The first Design Copyright Act was passed in 1839, securing copyright for a twelve month period after the article itself, or an illustration or model of it, had been deposited with the Design Registry of the Board of Trade. This Act related to all textile fabrics not covered by previous Acts, as well as the ornamentation, shape or configuration of most other manufactured articles, for a period of twelve months. The scope of the Act was considerably extended by subsequent legislation. For example, the 1839 Act made no allowance for functional, as opposed to decorative, designs, an anomaly put right by the 1845 Act which extended protection to all kinds of useful designs.

At the Register, design representations were glued into a book. Details of depositor's name, address and occupation were recorded in a separate register. Between 1842 and 1883 410,000 items were registered but in the much shorter period between 1884 and 1901, 368,154 were registered. However, the system would not seem to have been especially effective and it is clear that the designs of many businesses went unrecorded.

The Design Registry was originally maintained by the Board of Trade, but the function passed to the Patent Commissioners, subsequently the Patent Office, in 1875. Registers and representations of designs up to 1910 have been transferred to the Public Record Office. They are located in several series, but mostly classes BT 42–48, 50–53. Similar records of more recent date are kept in the Patent Office. Access to trade designs is by registration number and without this number the search for the designs of a given business is almost impossible. Some indexes to proprietors' names exist at BT 44/33–38, BT 46/5–7, BT 48/2 but most indexes would seem to have been destroyed. Many designs are registered in the name of the designer and not the manufacturer which makes searches that bit more difficult. No records arising out of pre-1839 legislation have survived.

The Public Record Office produces a three side leaflet called 'Design and Trade Marks: Registers and Representation' while a further useful reference is Sarah Levitt 'The Uses of Registered Design Samples in the Public Record Office, Kew, for the Study of Nineteenth Century Clothing Manufacturers', *Business Archives* 50, November 1984.

REPRESENTATIONS OF TRADE MARKS

Trade marks enable a trader to differentiate his products from those of others for the benefit of both the trader and the customer. The Trade Mark Registry came into being in January 1876, but almost immediately became part of the Patent Office. In 1876 over 10,000 trade marks were registered and since then the total number has risen to over one million.

Representations of trade marks up to 1938 have been deposited in the Public Record Office in class BT 82. Later records remain with the Patent Office. These do not reveal much useful information about a particular business but might, through painstaking research, provide the identity mark with which to identify the products of a business which are described elsewhere. The Patent Office's publication *A Century of Trade Marks* (London, 1976) provides more background information.

EXHIBITS IN COURTS OF LAW

The Public Record Office has numerous classes of exhibits which contain papers, accounts and other records of individuals, institutions and businesses, which were placed before various courts of law. These particular exhibits were for some reason never reclaimed and remained with the courts' administrators. The best known series are C 103 to C 114 but other classes include C 171, E 140, PL 12 and J 90. Some classes are extremely extensive; classes C 103 to C 114 contain 3,327 bundles of records dating from 1300 to 1800. E 140 contains 246 bundles ranging from the seventeenth to the nineteenth century. Various Court of Session classes in the Scottish Record Office contain similar records, most of which are held in CS 96. Some are listed in P L Payne *Studies in Scottish Business History* (London, 1967, pp 27–29).

Generally speaking these classes suffer from being catalogued many years ago, not in detail and often inaccurately. A considerable degree of interpretation is required. However, there is little doubt that excellent records are contained and this is confirmed by the contents of class J 90 which have recently been catalogued in considerable detail. The records of many businesses – banks, shipping firms, mines, engineering companies, publishers – are included. Class CS 96 in the Scottish Records Office is in process of being re-indexed. A helpful article on J 90 is John Orbell 'A Note on Series J 90 in the Public Record Office' *Business Archives*, November, 1983. The Public Record Office publishes a leaflet 'Chancery Proceedings (Equity Suits)' which outlines the records (and finding aids) of the Court of Chancery and the Supreme Court of Judicature.

BRITISH TRANSPORT HISTORICAL ARCHIVES

These archives were collected together in the late 1940s following the nationalisation of railway companies and have subsequently found their way into the Public Record Office (Kew) and the Scottish Record Office. The archives of well over 1000 railway and canal companies – many of the latter having been taken over by railway companies as a means of limiting competition – are contained in this collection. The diversity of materials ranges from minutes and accounts to timetables and operating publications. Generally the records of specific companies are arranged in individual classes (each with the prefix RAIL) but some classes are by type of record, for example annual reports of railway companies (RAIL 1110), railway company prospectuses (RAIL 1075–1076), canal company prospectuses (RAIL 1077), omnibus and other company prospectuses (RAIL 1078), agreements with companies for sidings (RAIL 1167), papers relating to welfare organisations (RAIL 1115), and so on. Some railway records, not selected for preservation by the PRO, may be deposited in local record offices.

Two early journal articles consider the collection before its arrival at the record offices: L C Johnson 'Historical Records in the British Transport Commission' *Journal of Transport History*, 1953, and L C Johnson 'British Transport Commission Archives: Work Since 1953' *Journal of Transport History*, 1962. A more wide ranging article, covering other PRO sources for railway history, is D B Wardle 'Sources for the History of Railways in the Public Record Office' *Journal of Transport History*, 1956. There is also a PRO leaflet 'British Transport Historical Records'.

REGISTRAR GENERAL OF SHIPPING AND SEAMEN

These records form part of the records of the Board of Trade and contain much information about British merchant shipping and seamen. They are of great use for studying the history of shipowners and builders. BT 107 to BT 110 contain four series of Transcripts and Transactions with an index in BT 111. These provide details of ownership, name, home port, place and date of building, and other details of British registered ships from 1814 onward (from 1786 in the case of the Port of London). Other classes include crew agreements and crew lists. Those for 1835 to 1860, together with some earlier ones for ships registered at a few other ports, are in BT 98. From 1861 a ten per cent sample has been retained in class BT 99 while a further ten per cent are in the National Maritime Museum and most of the rest are at the Memorial University of Newfoundland, St John's, Newfoundland. Others are in local record offices. From 1850 these classes also include official logs but these are largely a record of crew illness, punishment, desertion, etc. These and several other classes of records of the Registrar General are discussed in Nicholas Cox 'The Records of the Registrar General of Shipping and Seamen' *Maritime History*, 11, 1972. A leaflet 'Records of the Registrar General of Shipping and Seamen' is published by the PRO.

A note should also be given here about the records of Lloyds Register of Shipping deposited at Guildhall Library. They include Captain's Registers (1868–1947); *Lloyd's List* (1740–1970); Loss and Casualty Books (1837–1970); Subscription Books (1774–1849); *Lloyds Weekly Shipping Index* (1880–1917) giving details of ship voyages and casualty reports; and Lloyds Confidential Index (1886–c1950) giving lists of owners, details of ship sales and purchases, and loss record. These are described in C A Hall *A Guide to the Lloyd's Marine Collection at Guildhall Library* (Guildhall Library, 1985).

APPRENTICESHIP RECORDS

These form a further source of fairly limited information about a mass of businesses and businessmen. The Statutes of Apprenticeship, between 1563 and 1814, made it a requirement for every tradesman to serve an apprenticeship before practising his trade. In 1710 stamp duty became payable by masters on indentures of apprenticeship and for the years 1711 to 1808 the Commissioners of Stamps kept registers of money received and these are held in the Inland Revenue records in class IR 1. These record name of apprentice; date of indenture; details of master; and details of parents until 1752. Indexes of apprentices and masters are available in classes IR 1 and IR 17 for most registers (see below). However, many masters did not have to pay duty, for example when apprentices were taken on at the common or public charge. Between 1929 and 1941 the Society of Genealogists prepared indexes, arranged by name of apprentice, for the years 1711 to 1774, and by name of master, for the years 1710 to 1762. Copies of both indexes are available at Guildhall Library, the Society of Genealogists, and the PRO. The latter also publishes a leaflet called 'Apprenticeship Records as Sources for Genealogy in the Public Record Office'.

COMPANIES COURT OF THE HIGH COURT OF JUSTICE

The Public Record Office contains several classes of papers arising out of the work of the Companies Court. This court was concerned with hearing petitions and making judgements concerning the winding up of registered companies and changes in the constitution of companies as embodied in their memorandum and articles of association – eg alteration of a company's objects, reduction of its share capital, cancellation of certain shareholder rights, and so on. Much of this information will inevitably be held on the files of the Register of Companies and, in the case of quoted companies, in the records of the Stock Exchange. However, many files will relate to private companies whose returns to the Registers of Companies may not have survived.

The most extensive series by far is J 13 which consists of over 14,000 files relating to the winding up of companies, reductions of capital, alteration of shareholders' rights, etc. These contain copies of petitions, orders and judges' notes. The series dates from 1891 but from 1949 only a representative selection has been preserved. J 100 comprises Court books containing summaries of proceedings before the Court in the years 1919 to 1956. J 119 contains Registers of Petitions for the years c 1892 to 1949 while J 107 contains notes of the Court's Registrars. Series C 26 contains almost 700 files of proceedings and accounts in winding up actions.

Records of Associations

EMPLOYERS' ORGANISATIONS AND TRADE ASSOCIATIONS

This diverse group of organisations represents the interests of specific industries, either at a local or, more commonly, at a national level. Each organisation is funded through the subscriptions of member companies which determine policy.

Historically the functions of employers' organisations and trade associations differ fundamentally, although the present trend is towards the combination of functions into one organisation. Trade associations, at least at a national level, emerged in the last quarter of the nineteenth century although there were many shorter lived, regional associations in the early nineteenth century. In most cases their function was to fix prices and production quotas. Some had other reasons for formation. The Timber Trade Federation (established 1892) enabled its members to negotiate inland freight charges more effectively while the Society of Motor Manufacturers and Traders (established 1902) was concerned with the organisation of the Motor Show. The function of representing and speaking for the interests of an industry began to emerge during the First World War when industries needed to negotiate with government on such matters as regulation of production, expansion of strategic plant, supply of raw materials, and so on. Since 1956, when price fixing was made illegal, Trade Associations have strengthened their role in monitoring government policy and proposed legislation, providing economic and market intelligence, compiling technical publications, organising exhibitions and trade missions and, not least, making representations to the government and its agencies.

In contrast Employers' Organisations have been involved in the fixing of wages and conditions of employment and emerged in the late nineteenth century as a response to increasingly effective trade unions and in the early twentieth century as a consequence of the establishment of Wages Boards. Their original function was the regulation of wages and conditions of work across an industry. This was enhanced under wartime conditions and the arrival of industry-wide pay settlements. Many organisations still conduct industry-wide negotiations on wage rates and conditions but now also provide advice to members on wage trends, dispute procedures, productivity matters, and so on.

The records of Employers' Organisations and Trade Associations – largely minutes, files of papers, and publications – shed much light on the environment in which a business operated and the performance of the industry as a whole. However, it is reasonable to expect there to be information relating to individual businesses. Data for capacity, output, prices and costs would have been essential for the operation of any price fixing and production quota scheme. Details of labour costs, working conditions, size of workforce and so on would also have been collected for the regulation of wages.

The Modern Records Centre of the University of Warwick accommodates a growing collection of records of these organisations and they are described in Richard Storey and Alistair Tough *Consolidated Guide to the Modern Records Centre* (Coventry, 1986) and its predecessor publications Richard Storey and Janet Druker *Guide to the Modern Records Centre* (Coventry, 1977) and Richard Storey and Susan Edwards *Supplement to the Guide to the Modern Records Centre* (Coventry, 1981). H Campbell McMurray 'The Records of the Shipbuilders' and Repairers' National Association' *Business Archives*, November 1979, provides an in-depth description of a specimen collection housed in the National Maritime Museum. Over 30 books or articles on the history of specific bodies are listed in the Business Archives Council's *Broadsheet* No 4 'Bibliography of Histories of Employers' and Trade Organisations' (January 1979) compiled by Richard Storey. G S Bain and G B Woolven *A Bibliography of British Industrial Relations* (Cambridge, 1979) is also helpful.

The Confederation of British Industry (CBI) stands at the head of British industrial and commercial representation and traces its origins to three organisations established between 1915 and 1919 – the National Association of British Manufacturers, Federation of British Industries (FBI) and British Employers' Confederation. The records of these are also held at the Modern Records Centre and are described in Michael Wilcox *The Confederation of British Industry Predecessor Archive* (Coventry, 1984). An unpublished history of the FBI by Peter Mathias, written in the late 1960s, is available for study at the Centre and at the Business History Unit at the London School of Economics.

Trade Associations and Employers' Organisations are listed in the *Directory of British Associations* (1st edition 1965, 8th edition 1986) which provides address, date of formation, details of publications, etc, and has a subject index. Patricia Millard (ed) *Trade Associations and Professional Bodies of the United Kingdom* (1st edition 1962, 7th edition 1985) is a similar publication but provides less detail.

STOCK EXCHANGES

Records of stock exchanges will shed light both on the companies whose shares were quoted on these exchanges and on the stock-brokers who were members of them. Simply put, a stock exchange is a market place where investors buy and sell shares and other se-curities through the medium of stockbrokers. By far the most important British stock exchange is in London (formally consti-tuted in 1802) but in the 1980s provincial offices also exist at Belfast, Birmingham, Bristol, Glasgow, Liverpool and Manchester which trace their origins as independent stock exchanges to the 1830s or 1840s. Provincial stock exchanges also existed from the nineteenth century until recent years at Sheffield, Leeds, Newcastle, Hull, York, Huddersfield, Nottingham, Halifax, Edinburgh, Aberdeen, Leicester and elsewhere. In 1973 all United Kingdom stock exchanges amalgamated to form the Stock Exchange.

In its early days the London Stock Exchange was largely concerned with British and overseas government bonds. It was not until the formation of joint stock companies, from the 1820s but especially from the 1840s, that it developed an important corporate function. Companies whose shares are listed on the Stock Exchange are, almost by definition, public companies as opposed to private companies whose shares are not listed.

Information contained in the archives of the London Stock Exchange – held at Guildhall Library – relates to the initial listing of a company's shares and to listing of subsequent share issues; to enquiries mounted by the Stock Exchange into suspicious dealings in shares, for example the creation of a false market in a company's shares, into inaccurate performance forecasts made at the time of initial listing and so on; and to details surrounding the suspension of trading in a company's shares. Details of share price movements are also useful in giving a broad indication of performance.

Guildhall Library holds many thousands of 'applications for listing' files supported by a card index finding aid arranged in alphabetical order of name of company. The content of these files varies over the years in accordance with the Stock Exchange's requirements but even those before 1900 contain a letter of application for listing giving details of the company's objects, capital, voting rights, procedure for increasing capital, borrowing powers and so on. These are invariably supported by articles of association, prospectus, specimen letter of allotment and share certificate, bankers' voucher giving name of bankers, agreements concerning assets acquired by the company, and so on. The files cover the years 1850 to 1926 while more recent files are held by the Stock Exchange. Many of these papers will also have been filed with the Registers of Companies but not all. The records deposited with Guildhall Library are held in an outstore (in 1986) and 24 hours notice of use of a file is needed. Therefore two separate visits to the Guildhall are necessary, one to consult the card index and the other to study the file itself. Quoted companies had to file at least one copy of their annual report with the Stock Exchange and these are also held at Guildhall Library. They are described in the section on Annual Reports (see page 70).

Details of London Stock Exchange members (ie stock brokers or jobbers) are held in the 148 volumes of Applications for Admission to Membership which cover the years 1802 to 1901 and in a Register of New Applicants, 1886–1903. From 1836 printed lists of members and firms – *S E Members and Firms* – are available at Guildhall Library.

Records of some provincial stock exchanges have also been deposited in record offices, for example those of Sheffield Stock Exchange covering the years 1850 to 1974 in Sheffield Central Library; Leeds Stock Exchange from 1845 to 1934 in Leeds City Library; Glasgow Stock Exchange in Glasgow University Archives; and Aberdeen Stock Exchange for the nineteenth century in Aberdeen University Library.

Lists, ie printed daily sheets giving details of share or bond price movements, were published, often under authority of stock exchanges. They are useful in so far as they give an indication of the perceived performance of a company. In London *The Course of Exchange* was published between 1697 and 1908. By the 1880s it already carried sections on banks, insurance companies, telegraph and telephone companies, gas companies, and others. Other useful publications giving details of Stock Exchange prices and other information are the *Stock Exchange Daily Official List* (from 1863), the *Stock Exchange Weekly Intelligence* (from 1869) and the *Stock Exchanges, London and Provincial, 10 Year Record* (from 1897). Guildhall Library has a particularly good collection of Stock Exchange publications. In the twentieth century the national press has recorded daily stock exchange prices.

W A Thomas *The Provincial Stock Exchanges. Their History and Function* (London, 1973) and W A Thomas *Stock Exchanges of Ireland* (Liverpool, 1986) are useful reading. The former describes briefly the runs of minutes and 'lists' of provincial exchanges used by the author. There are many histories of the London Stock Exchange of which the most helpful is E Victor Morgan and W A Thomas *The Stock Exchange. Its History and Function* (London, 1962). R C Michie *Money, Mania and Markets* (Edinburgh, 1981) considers stock exchanges, brokers and investment in Scotland.

CHAMBERS OF COMMERCE AND TRADE

Chambers of commerce represent the interests of manufacturers, merchants, service industries and distributive trades in a geographical area, while chambers of trade are composed mainly or entirely of businesses engaged in distribution in a geographical area. By 1850 most industrial cities and large towns had formed their own chamber but only a very few chambers could trace their origins to the late eighteenth century. Numbers rose rapidly in the late Victorian period. In the late 1970s 10 regional and 90 local chambers of commerce and over 800 chambers of trade existed.

In 1858 the functions of chambers were described as: promoting measures for the benefit of the local business community; representing the interests of this community in local affairs; collecting data concerning local industry; and settling disputes between members. Today chambers continue to provide a forum in which local business can discuss issues of mutual importance and then make representations, especially to local authorities. They also provide members with a wide range of practical services: issue of certificates of origin, organisation of trade missions, provision of telex and translation facilities, and so on.

As with the records of trade and employer associations, chambers of commerce records will provide details about the conditions – essentially local ones – under which a business operated. They invariably consist of minutes and membership records which, if nothing else, will indicate if a local business, and its leaders, played an active role in local business affairs. The most extensive collection is probably that of the London Chamber of Commerce. Its archives, at Guildhall Library, contain a very large number of minute books for its many sections representing businesses involved in a particular industry or in trading to a particular geographical area. They include, for example, minute books of the Cement Trade Section (1889–1909), the Bristle Trade Section (1928–61), the Chemical Trades Section (1883–1926), the China and Glass Retailers' Association (1915–56), the Russian Section (1908–64), the East African Section (1920–58), and so on. Membership records include ten volumes of subscription registers for 1884–1959; registers of resignations which include reasons for resignation for 1910–71; and registers of new members for 1912–71.

Over twenty collections of chambers of commerce records are described in Lesley Richmond and Bridget Stockford *Company Archives* (Aldershot, 1986).

TRADE UNIONS

In understanding a business the contribution of its workforce is a crucial, yet often understated, consideration. The records of organised labour, existing in quantity from the late nineteenth century, are most obviously helpful in shedding light on the nature of the workforce, for example education, age, health and sex; on wages and benefits; on working conditions; on attitudes of management to labour and vice versa; and on industrial actions and their effect. This information will generally relate to an industrial sector as a whole rather than to individual businesses.

The exceptions are when, perhaps, those businesses are particularly large or significant in relation to specific issues such as unionisation, disputes, introduction of new technology and redundancies. Records may also contain general information on financial performance, sales, productivity and outlook, for industrial sectors if not for particular businesses.

By far the best collection of trade union records is deposited in the Modern Records Centre of the University of Warwick. The Centre produces a range of helpful guides of which the most important are mentioned in the section on Employers' Organisations and Trade Associations. A further Centre publication, *Trade Union and Related Records* (Coventry, 3rd ed, 1983), is a guide to primary sources in the UK for trade union history. Joyce M Bellamy and John Saville (eds) *The Dictionary of Labour Biography* (London, 1972–), published in several volumes and replete with footnotes giving details of primary and secondary sources, is also helpful. Arthur Marsh and Victoria Ryan *Historical Directory of Trade Unions* (Aldershot, 1980–) provides short histories, of about 100 to 300 words, of trade unions, and also gives details of source material. Four volumes are planned of which three had been published by 1987. For Scotland there is Ian MacDougall *A Catalogue of Some Labour Records in Scotland and Some Scottish Records Outside Scotland* (Scottish Labour History Society, Edinburgh, 1978).

MARKET ORGANISATIONS

Stock exchanges are one form of market organisation but many

64

others exist which are of local or national importance. Their records, besides giving details of their members and of businesses who traded in the markets, will indicate prevailing prices, trading conditions and the business environment generally. The archives of several market organisations are described in Lesley Richmond and Bridget Stockford *Company Archives* (Aldershot, 1986).

Corn exchanges are perhaps the most numerous type of market organisation and their records are deposited in large quantities in local record offices. At the other extreme markets of national significance include the Baltic Exchange and the London Metal Exchange (both of which have retained their archives), the Covent Garden Vegetable and Flower Market (archives at Greater London Record Office), the Smithfield Meat Market and the Billingsgate Fish Market (both archives at the Corporation of London Record Office).

LIVERY COMPANIES

The livery companies of the City of London have existed from medieval times. Their records are particularly useful as they refer to business activity before modern times when there is a dearth of source material. Livery companies were social and religious bodies in origin but also acquired economic functions by regulating and indeed monopolising particular trades or crafts. Their regulatory authority flourished until the sixteenth, seventeenth and eighteenth centuries when they began to decline as trade or craft guilds. Archives dating back to at least the eighteenth century exist for over eighty companies; the earliest document was created in the twelfth century and half the companies have material created before 1500.

Many records relate to the administration of the companies' affairs but, for those seeking details of individual businesses, membership and apprenticeship records are the most useful. Apprenticeship registers, some of which exist for as early as the fifteenth century, may include name of apprentice; date of presentment; father's name; age; place of origin; length of apprenticeship; and details of master. In addition there are useful records of regulation of trade and craft practices, which generally meant the identification of inferior produce or dishonest weights and measures. Regulatory powers of most livery companies were restricted to the City of London but some companies had a national authority. Best known is the function of the Goldsmiths' Company for assaying and marking gold and silver, and of the Stationers' Company which had a national monopoly for registration of printed books. Mark Books, containing the 'trade mark' of individual craftsmen, enable identification of the products of the members of some companies.

Livery companies were restricted to the City of London but other ancient cities and towns also had associations of tradesmen and merchants. York, for example, has two surviving to the present day – the Merchant Taylors' Company and the Merchant Adventurers' Company. Associations of merchants include the East India Association of Glasgow, whose archives for 1812 to 1963 are held by the Mitchell Library, Glasgow, and the Society of Merchant Venturers of Bristol, whose records from 1639 to the nineteenth century are in Bristol University Library.

An excellent guide to livery company records is C R H Cooper 'The Archives of the City of London Livery Companies and Related Organisations' while the records of a single company are discussed in Susan M Hare 'The Records of the Goldsmiths' Company'. Both articles may be found in *Archives* 72 (Oct 1984). The surviving records (especially relating to membership) of many provincial guilds have been published by local history societies.

Printed Sources

PUBLISHED HISTORIES

Many businesses, including ones that have become defunct in recent years, have either published a printed history, in hardback or pamphlet form, or have produced a typed fact sheet outlining major events in their history. These are useful as gifts for customers and suppliers as a marketing or public relations exercise. The earliest histories were published in the late nineteenth century, more were produced between the wars, but since the 1950s there has been a flood. Publication often marks an anniversary and books are celebratory rather than academic in approach. As an alternative, an article on a business's history at the time of an anniversary might appear in the trade press (see page 77) or house journal (see page 76) or local newspaper (see page 71). As so many company histories, and indeed biographies of businessmen, are privately printed, they are often difficult to locate in public and academic libraries. Nevertheless it is always worth looking up the company name, and names of partners or directors, in the British Library catalogue. It is surprising what can be found.

The journal, *Business History*, includes many articles covering the history of specific businesses. The superb five volume *Dictionary of Business Biography* (London, 1984–86), ably edited by David Jeremy, covers the careers of 1000 leading businessmen at work between 1860 and 1980. The two volume *Dictionary of Scottish Business Biography* (Aberdeen, 1986–87) covers 500 Scottish businessmen whose careers span the years 1860 to 1960.

The Business Archives Council maintains a rapidly expanding

library of well over 4500 histories (3000 books and 1500 pamphlets) and is recognised as the best collection in Britain. Useful collections are also at Bristol University Library and Guildhall Library. *The Shorter Aslib Directory of Information Sources in the United Kingdom* (London, 1986) is the most useful guide to the resources of both public and private (including company) libraries.

Since 1969 the Business Archives Council's journal, *Business Archives*, has included a list of business histories published in the previous year, although because of the large number of private publications it does not claim to be comprehensive. In the mid–1980s the Business History Unit at the London School of Economics embarked upon the preparation of an extensive bibliography of printed histories, published under the title Francis Goodall *Bibliography of British Business Histories* (Aldershot, 1987). J M Bellamy *Yorkshire Business Histories. A Bibliography* (Bradford, 1970) provides a particularly detailed guide to published works and articles on businesses in Yorkshire while D J Rowe *Northern Business Histories. A Bibliography* (London, 1979) gives similar coverage to Cumbria, Durham and Northumberland. P L Payne *Studies in Scottish Business History* (London 1967) contains a 21 page bibliography of Scottish business histories, but many outstanding histories of Scottish businesses have appeared since its publication. A few published bibliographies cover specific industrial sectors, the most ambitious of which is George Ottley *A Bibliography of British Railway History* (London, 2nd edition 1983).

ANNUAL REPORTS

Every company has a need to report on its performance and to explain profits, and especially losses, to those who have invested money in its shares, or might do so in the future. A company reports to its shareholders by means of circulating an annual report and accounts which is commented on and approved at annual general meetings. Invariably this is printed and, today, extends to several pages, especially in the case of public companies. Prior to 1945 the annual report was often a much briefer document.

Historically, the existence of an annual report depended more on a company's policy than on the requirements of company law or, in the case of quoted companies, of the Stock Exchange. The 1845 Company Act simply stipulated that a company's directors should produce a balance sheet and auditor's report to shareholders attending the annual general meeting. The 1856 and 1862 Acts did not establish any statutory obligation although the model articles of association stated that a printed copy of a balance sheet laid before an annual general meeting should be sent in advance and by post to each shareholder. The 1907 Act was no more explicit, although it did stipulate that the balance sheet submitted to the annual general meeting was to be sent to the Register of Companies. The 1929 Act for the first time stipulated that in the case of public companies a copy of every balance sheet laid before an annual general meeting should be sent to all shareholders prior to the annual general meeting. In the case of a private company any shareholder who made application to the company had to be sent the balance sheet. The 1948 Act confirmed these arrangements but also stipulated that the profit and loss account presented to the annual general meeting (a requirement of the 1929 Act) also had to be circulated. Notwithstanding this legislation many companies, especially public ones, elected to send annual balance sheets and an explanatory report to shareholders. This requirement was invariably embodied in the company's articles of association, and from 1906 the London Stock Exchange insisted that this was done, as a condition for the quotation of shares and for the protection of investors. In 1929, in the wake of the Hatry affair, the Exchange insisted on the supply of fuller information to investors and this included the addition of a profit and loss account to the annual report.

The content of annual reports varied enormously both over time and between companies. In the nineteenth century they might consist only of a balance sheet and a short report containing brief corporate details such as the appointment or resignation of directors. At the other extreme they could extend to several pages and give descriptions of the company's assets, details of sales backed by tables of statistics, information about major investment decisions, and explanations for good or poor performance. They can be extremely helpful documents but an element of cautious interpretation is required in their reading.

Active companies invariably retain a complete file of past annual reports, often stuck into minute books. Throughout their history copies might have been lodged with the Registers of Companies but this was not always the case especially as the information which had to be disclosed to shareholders need not necessarily be the same as that which had to be reported to the Registers. The Stock Exchange received copies of annual reports from quoted companies and these were used for compiling the *Stock Exchange Year Book* (see page 3). This collection is now housed in Guildhall Library. The reports are arranged in *Stock Exchange Year Book* order, although some categories are subdivided, eg plantation companies under tea, coffee or rubber. Miscellaneous companies are bound as commercial. The series commences in 1880 and the first reports, 1880–85, are bound together. Those for 1886 to 1964/65 are bound annually. The reports for 1880 to 1885 are very incomplete and the arrangement of companies can be erratic. Two days notice of use is required for ordering volumes.

Useful discussions about the reliability and content of the account sections of annual reports are contained in J R Edwards *Company Legislation and Changing Patterns of Disclosure in British Company Accounts 1900–1940* (The Institute of Chartered Accountants in England and Wales, 1981) and Sheila Marriner 'Company Financial Statements as Source Material for Business Historians' *Business History*, 1980.

PROSPECTUSES

When a company advertises its shares, debentures or other securities for sale, either when it is first formed or when it needs to increase its capital, it issues a prospectus. As well as providing details of the shares and other securities for sale, the prospectus gives background information about the company including details of its assets and its performance in, say, the previous decade.

Guildhall Library houses a valuable collection of company prospectuses, deposited by the Stock Exchange, covering the years 1824 to 1963. It is comprehensive. Those for 1824 to 1880 are bound in one alphabetical sequence while from 1881 to 1963 they are bound annually. Microfiche copies are available of the years 1824 to 1901.

Prospectuses, especially in recent years, have also been published in the national press, especially in *The Financial Times* and *The Times*. *The Extel Book of Prospectuses and New Issues* is a compilation of public prospectuses of new companies and established companies issuing further tranches of securities. It was first published by *The Times* in 1891 and has been known under a number of titles, including *The Times Book of Prospectuses*. In 1986 the publication appeared in microfiche form for the first time.

NEWSPAPERS

Local and national newspapers contain a wealth of information about businesses, eg reports on rebuilding and extension of factories, offices and other plant, accidents such as floods and fires, large contracts won, works outings, strikes, etc. They might contain obituaries of businessmen, especially if these men were prominent in local affairs. Advertisements of products and sale particulars of business premises are also carried. The latter can be particularly useful in giving details of capacity, size, machinery, layout, and so on. National newspapers, such as *The Times* and *The Financial Times*, published detailed accounts of the proceedings of general meetings of public companies as well as reporting on annual results. *The Economist* (first published 1843), *The Statist* (first published 1878) and *The Investors' Chronicle* (first published 1860 as *The Money Market Review*) are also of obvious use but mostly cover the affairs of public companies. All have helpful indexes.

The usefulness of newpapers is tempered by the general absence of name and subject indexes which can make a search for details of a particular business like looking for a needle in a haystack. *The Times* is a notable exception, and a name and subject index for each year of publication has been published since 1787. These are increasingly detailed over time, especially from 1906 when the *Official Index to The Times* was first published, and are available in any good reference library, as indeed is *The Times*. The *Glasgow Herald* published an index between 1903 and 1979 and an indexing project covering *The Scotsman* is underway. An index of *The Financial Times* was published between 1913 and 1920 in 92 monthly parts and since 1982 an index of contents has been resumed on a regular basis. *Research Index*, published by Business Surveys Ltd since 1965, is an index to articles and news items, arranged by subject and company name, appearing in a wide selection of periodicals and in the national press. Some provincial newspapers have been indexed by local historians and more recently by Manpower Services Commission Schemes. These include *The Newcastle Courant*, *The Gateshead Observer* and other North East newspapers, *The Cambridge Chronicle*, *The Nottingham Journal* and *The York Courant*. These are not published but are available in card index form in reference libraries at Gateshead, Cambridge, Nottingham and York. When no index exists a researcher needs approximate dates of events in order to search for any newspaper reports which might have appeared. Most local history libraries have runs of local newspapers, sometimes in microfilm form. The British Library Newspaper Library has the national newspaper collection with comprehensive runs of London, provincial, Scottish and Irish newspapers, as well as of major newspapers published abroad. An eight volume catalogue is published. There is also a published index of Scottish newspapers – Joan P S Ferguson *Dictionary of Scottish Newspapers* (National Library of Scotland, Edinburgh, 1984). A general bibliography of the British press, which gives details of published indexes, is David Linton and Ray Boston (eds) *The Newspaper Press in Britain: An Annotated Bibliography* (London, 1987). John West *Town Records* (Chichester, 1983) provides a gazetteer, arranged by town, of what local newspapers have been published since 1690.

TRADE DIRECTORIES

Trade directories list the name, address and business activity of some or all businesses in a given locality or for a given industrial sector. Geographical directories cover either a county or city or town while sector directories cover an industry or trade. The principal function of both was to put customers and suppliers in touch with producers of goods and services, and *vice versa*.

Geographical directories are one of the most important sources for obtaining basic details of a late eighteenth or early nineteenth-century business. The first, covering London, was published in 1677 and there is a copy at Guildhall Library. The next were published in 1734 and 1735, also for London, but no copies appear to have survived. The first provincial directories were published in the 1770s – for Liverpool, Manchester and Bristol. Hampshire had the first county directory in 1784 (again no copy survives). *Bailey's British Directory*, published in four volumes in 1784, and the *Universal British Directory*, published in parts between 1791 and 1798, were on a more ambitious scale and covered many medium and small sized towns as well as large commercial and industrial centres. However, serious grounds exist for doubting their accuracy. It was not really until after the early decades of the nineteenth century that directories were published for most counties, cities and large towns which were accurate and revised frequently if not annually. Early directories, based on inefficient means of data collection, were notoriously inaccurate and were not comprehensive, covering just the principal traders rather than all traders. Kelly's *Post Office Directory of London*, first published in 1836, was a pointer to things to come. Like an increasing number of directories, it was published annually, was accurate and contained three sections: an alphabetical list of businesses, lists of businesses classified according to trade, and lists of businesses according to the street in which they were based.

When directories began to give comprehensive lists of businesses and were revised and republished at fairly frequent intervals, then details of changes in name, address and activity can be discerned. Moreover, the first mention of a business in a series of annual directories *might* well indicate year of formation while the last mention *might* indicate year of liquidation. From the mid-nineteenth century other information contained *might* give details of goods sold or manufactured, the location of other factories or shops, the award of prizes for product excellence, whether the business was a government contractor, agencies held, and so on.

73

Such entries are, however, very much the exception as they had to be paid for by the business concerned.

Local history libraries and record offices often have a very full collection of directories relating to the areas they serve. Guildhall Library has an excellent collection, not just for London but for the country as a whole. The National Art Library, based at the Victoria and Albert Museum, also has a fine collection of over 1000 volumes which is described in Michael E Keen *A Bibliography of the Trade Directories... in the National Art Library* (Victoria and Albert Museum, 1979). Another useful publication, despite its early date, is Jane E Norton *Guide to National and Provincial Directories of England and Wales, Excluding London, Published Before 1856* (Royal Historical Society, 1950). Not only does this indicate the location of directories, it makes useful general comments about accuracy. For London CWF Goss *The London Directories 1677–1855* (London, 1932) and P J Atkins *The Directories of London 1677–1914* (University of Durham, computer printout, 1981) are helpful in indicating what is available. The Department of Geography at Exeter University is in the process of compiling a computer based list of British directories, whether national or local, geographical or industrial sector, published between 1850 and 1950. In 1986 the database contained details of over 1600 directories held in eight major libraries.

Industrial sector directories – again a source for putting customers, suppliers and producers in touch with one another – are extremely diverse in their content, both between publications and over time. When detailed they can be extremely useful. Generally speaking, very many were first published in the last decades of the nineteenth century.

A few examples serve to illustrate the diversity of their content and their usefulness. *The Chemical Manufacturers' Directory*, published annually from 1867 until 1963, in 1914 provided little more than a list of manufacturers, giving name of business, address(es) and product(s) made. Nevertheless, an analysis of the whole series would provide useful information about changes in the products manufactured by a given company over time. A list of manufacturers, classified according to product manufactured, is also given and there are many informative advertisements placed either by chemical manufacturers or suppliers to the industry. At a different extreme is *The Railway Year Book*, published from 1898 until 1932. The 1923 edition, for example, includes for each railway company names and addresses of directors; names of principal managers and engineers; a history with details of acquisitions and subsidiary companies; information about length of track and rolling stock; and statistics of business and financial performance. A further section covers overseas railway companies, especially those which were British owned, while a third section provides short biographies of leading railway managers. *Railway Intelligence* covered similar information for the years 1849 to 1879. A further example is *The Bankers' Almanac*, published from 1845. As well as giving a great deal of practical information about banking it provided, in 1845, lists of active banks and details of year of establishment; number of partners or shareholders; paid up capital and share price in the case of joint stock banks; location of branches; size of bank note issue; name of London agent; and so on. By the end of the century details of published balance sheets are also included. *Fairplay's Annual Summary of British Shipping Finance* by the 1940s was giving for each British shipping company details of directors, principal shareholders and managers; brief details of size of fleet; and details of published balance sheets. It was published between 1925 and 1951.

The Red Book of Commerce or Who's Who in Business (London, annually 1906–39) is worth a special comment. This is neither a geographical nor a trade directory; it is a directory of British businesses, large and small, involved in a very wide range of activities. The basis for inclusion is not clear but the 1906 issue contained about 2000 entries and that for 1920, about 5000. A typical entry is 200 words long and gives details of function, products, address, hours of business, date of establishment, previous trading names, number of employees, present directors or partners, and a short history of the business. By comparing issue with issue a fairly detailed picture of the business can be built up.

As well as geographical and trade directors, from the late nineteenth century a number of directories of individual businessmen were published. For example Herbert H Bassett *Business Men at Home and Abroad. A Biographical Directory of Partners, Principals, Directors and Managers of Important Firms and*

Institutions of Home and Abroad (London, 1912–13) gives brief details of over 5000 businessmen. A glance at the British Library Catalogue under 'Directories General' indicates the range of directories available.

No guide has been published covering directory publications, so finding those for a given industry might require a good deal of research. *Willing's Press Guide* (first published 1874), an annual publication listing periodicals and newspapers, is helpful, especially the subject classification section. However, back copies are hard to come by. *The Newspaper Press Directory* (first published 1849 and now known as *Benn's Media Directory*) is a similar publication. Complete sets of both publications can be found on the open shelves of the British Library Newspaper Library at Colindale, London. *The Waterloo Directory of Victorian Periodicals 1824–1900* (University of Waterloo and Wilfred Laurier University Press, 1976), available in good reference libraries, is helpful but lacks a subject index. *The British Union Catalogue of Periodicals. A Record of The Periodicals of the World from the Seventeenth Century to the Present Day in British Libraries* (4 vols, London, 1955–58, and subsequent supplements) is most helpful, especially in indicating where periodicals are located but it also lacks a subject index. The computer based index of directories compiled at Exeter University, includes some references to sector directories.

HOUSE JOURNALS

These are the staff newspapers or magazines produced by companies and circulated amongst their employees. Often they are printed and illustrated but otherwise are duplicated typescripts and take the form of a newsletter. Their function is to inform employees of activities within their company or group of companies. *Progress*, the house journal of Lever Brothers Ltd, when first published in 1900, had as its aim 'intercommunication between the head office and works at Port Sunlight, the branch offices in the United Kingdom and the offices and agencies, oil mills and affiliated companies abroad'. Most house journals are a product of the post 1945 years but a few date back to the late nineteenth century. In 1964 it was estimated that 1800 were being published, a figure which has undoubtedly risen.

Progress provides a useful example of the content of early journals. It contained information about staff social activities and promotions; staff benefits such as bonuses and profit sharing; management philosophy; advertising campaigns; new products; prizes won; opening, amalgamation or closure of sites of operation; and so on. *Progress* had nothing to report on financial performance in its early years. News of financial performance, and explanations for it, are a feature of many post-war journals. Another example is the journal of Metal Box plc, *Metal Box News*, first published in 1952. The contents of the first issues included many details of social and sports functions, notices of retirements and obituaries but also an account of the Chairman's visit to subsidiaries in India and Australia; a profile of the Metal Box Co. of India Ltd; details of the company's presentation at The Packaging Exhibition; photographs of new product lines; a history of the company's 50-year association with Worcester; and details of the commissioning of a strip mill.

House journals were privately published and, therefore, did not automatically find their way into copyright libraries – the British Library, National Libraries of Scotland and Wales, Universities of Oxford and Cambridge, etc. This said the Reference Library of the British Library (based at the British Museum) has several and there are many others in the British Library Newspaper Library at Colindale, London and in the Trade Literature Collection of the Science Reference Library, a further branch of the British Library, at Holborn, London.

At least some nineteenth-century house journals are listed in *The Waterloo Directory of Victorian Periodicals* while *The British Union Catalogue of Periodicals* is also helpful but lists only those which have entered major library collections. These publications are described in the entry on Directories. An especially useful publication is the British Association of Industrial Editors *British House Journals* (London, 1956) which lists over 700 companies publishing house journals in 1956. The Association may be a useful source of general advice concerning house journals.

TRADE PRESS

A wide range of periodical literature has been published, mostly by commercial publishers, for the consumption of managers at work in specific industries or business sectors. The range of periodicals is almost limitless and several can exist for the same industry, being differentiated in terms of commercial and technical content. A very few periodicals were published in the early nineteenth century but most appeared in the last decades of that century.

Some specimen publications indicate the diversity of periodicals and information available. *The Country Brewers' Gazette*, known subsequently as *The Brewers' Gazette and Wine and Spirits Trades' Journal*, published between 1877 and 1931, at the end of the nineteenth century contained reports of company annual general meetings; reports on law cases touching the brewing industry and often involving specific businesses; stock and share price performance of quoted companies; obituaries of leading figures in the industry; details of patents and trade marks registered; technical articles; and advertisements placed by suppliers to the industry. *The Draper and Clothier*, published between May 1859 and April 1862, was designed as an 'organ of intercommunication and permanent record of news, advertisements and information for... all manufacturers or dealers in textile fabrics'. A typical issue for 1859 contains details of 'new inventions and improvements'; correspondence with the editor; law reports; lists of bankruptcies and dissolutions presumably taken from *The London Gazette*; and advertisements including 'a list of drapery businesses and premises for disposal' placed by James Livett, a City accountant, giving details of situation, stock value, rental, 'returns', lease, sale price, etc, but these businesses are *not* identified. *Rubber Information*, first published in 1930, was directed at technical managers but again there are items of general information: lists of new trade marks; advertisements placed by suppliers to the industry; a classified list of manufacturers and suppliers of raw materials, products, plant and equipment; and trade statistics including tables giving details of performance of rubber plantation companies with name, issued capital, profit or loss, dividend, rubber acreage, acreage under coffee, year's rubber

78

crop, etc. Much, if not all, of this was presumably extracted from the annual reports of public companies but it is presented in a convenient and comparative form.

The trade press remains a very under-used source for historians. There are no survey articles or special bibliographies. *The Waterloo Directory of Victorian Periodicals* and *The British Union Catalogue of Periodicals* are useful in tracing periodicals available but no subject indexes to them exist. Fuller descriptions are provided in the entry on Directories.

TRADE CATALOGUES

These form the largest part of the mass of literature privately published by business organisations. Trade catalogues were, in effect, illustrated handbooks giving descriptions and sometimes prices of goods produced by a business. Often they contain photographs of installed capital equipment and of the business's own factory. They were printed, often had hard backs and could be several inches thick. They were circulated by manufacturers and/or wholesalers, and sometimes retailers, to prospective customers and covered such products as furniture, architectural ironmongery, sanitary ware, fireplaces, textiles, machine tools, other engineered products, seeds and fertilizers, and so on. In the same category as trade catalogues are exhibition catalogues, published in connection with major exhibitions of manufactured goods, the most notable of which were published for the Great Exhibition of 1851.

Although trade catalogues could be widely circulated, because they were privately published they were not deposited in copyright libraries. Therefore, the survival of a complete set for a given business is highly unlikely. The Trade Literature Collection of the Science Reference Library of the British Library might well be the best national collection, but it is very far from complete. The Science Museum Library and the Victoria and Albert Museum also have useful collections reflecting their areas of specialisation. Manchester Polytechnic held an exhibition of some of its collection of trade catalogues in May 1978 and published a short exhibition catalogue illustrating the breadth of material available – *Historical Trade Catalogues* (Manchester Polytechnic Library, 1978).

PARLIAMENTARY PAPERS

Government, both central and local, publishes a mass of material which has a bearing on business activity. Much is of interest to historians of business but the most important publication as a source of historical data is House of Commons Sessional Papers, more commonly known as Parliamentary Papers. This series, printed on a regular basis from 1801, is made up of over 12,000 volumes. It comprises three types of record: bills; reports and accounts of committees and Royal Commissions; and papers providing Parliament with data it has ordered to be presented for information purposes, often on a regular annual basis. Papers are of considerable interest and include data covering the performance of the economy as a whole as well as annual returns of data on a wide range of subjects including joint stock companies registration, saving banks, friendly societies, and so on. Reports of committees are also of considerable interest, those on different industries often containing evidence given by leading businessmen. Often they also contain useful tables of statistics.

Parliamentary Papers prior to 1801 were not published on a regular basis but in 1975–76 those papers presented between *c*1714 and 1800 were reprinted in 147 volumes by Scholarly Resources Ltd. The series includes a useful introduction to the pre–1801 material. Irish University Press in the late 1960s reprinted in about 1000 volumes the most interesting nineteenth-century papers. To both series there are contemporary and recent indexes. Notwithstanding reprinting projects, comprehensive sets of Parliamentary Papers are only found in leading academic and reference libraries. However, a Readex Microfilm copy is more generally available.

Parliamentary Papers, together with other government publications, are discussed in Frank Rodgers *A Guide to British Government Publications* (New York, 1980). Of more particular help is P & G Ford *A Guide to Parliamentary Papers* (3rd ed, Shannon, Ireland, 1972). The Fords have also written breviates of Parliamentary Papers which provide useful summaries (c 500 words) of objectives, deliberations, contents and conclusions of the more important committee reports and other publications. The Fords' works include *A Breviate of Parliamentary Papers 1900–1916* (Oxford, 1957), *A Breviate of Parliamentary Papers 1917–1939* (Oxford, 1951), and *A Breviate of Parliamentary Papers 1940–1954* (Oxford, 1961).

MAPS

Large scale maps, defined here as one inch or more to the mile, form an invaluable source for studying changes in the landscape and, from time to time, shed some light on businesses. They provide, for example, details of approximate size of buildings, layout of buildings, location relative to the transport system and to other industrial buildings, and so on.

The first one inch map of an entire English county was published in 1700 but it was between 1759 and 1809 that the first detailed and reliable one inch surveys were made of practically every English and many Scottish counties. These early maps marked various industrial buildings, especially when they were important features of the landscape such as windmills and watermills. Ordnance Survey maps, which were more accurate and detailed, were published from 1801 onwards, first for the South East. Most of England had been surveyed by the late 1830s and the whole of Britain by 1873. Until 1840 maps on the scale of one inch to the mile were published. The first six inch surveys, for Yorkshire and Lancashire, were published between 1840 and 1854. Six inch and 25 inch surveys were published for the rest of Britain between the late 1850s and the early 1890s. These are much more useful and show in detail the outline of industrial buildings and often give their name and function. The early one inch maps were based on field surveys on the scale of either two, three or six inches to the mile. From the late 1840s the scale was 25 inches to the mile. These drawings are lodged in the Map Library of the British Library and are available in microfiche form. They provide some details not found on the published maps and give survey date. This is important as this date was invariably several years before date of publication. From the 1850s onwards the Ordnance Survey also published town plans on particularly large scales, for example five feet and ten feet to the mile. The first towns thus covered were mostly based in Lancashire and Yorkshire but there was a good national spread by the 1890s.In addition to published maps, innumerable large scale manuscript maps were drawn for a variety of functions and local and national record offices have collections.

A useful source of reference to early maps is E M Rodger *The Large Scale County Maps of the British Isles 1596–1850. A Union List* (Oxford, 1972). J B Harley *The Historian's Guide to Ordnance Survey Maps* (The Standing Conference for Local History, 1964) is equally helpful. There is an excellent gazetteer of town maps and plans covering the years 1600 to 1900 in John West *Town Records* (Chichester, 1983). *Descriptive List of Plans in the Scottish Record Office* (3 vols, 1966–1974) and *Maps and Plans in the Public Record Office* (HMSO 1967) are also published. Ian Watt *A Directory of UK Map Collections* (Map Curators' Group Publication No 3, 1985) provides very brief details of map collections in British libraries and record offices.

The maps and plans of Chas E Goad Ltd are worthy of special mention. From the mid-1880s until the 1970s this firm produced large scale and very detailed maps of the major urban centres, largely for the use of fire insurance offices in calculating risk. 126 areas were mapped, almost entirely central business districts. The scale was generally one inch to 40 feet and revisions were made every five years or less. Properties are clearly demarcated and give name of company, product line and details of construction. Important collections are in the Map Library of the British Library, Guildhall Library and the major reference libraries. Useful reading is Gwyn Rowley 'British Fire Insurance Plans: The Goad Productions c1885–c1970' *Archives*, 1985 and Chas E Goad Ltd *Goad Fire Insurance Plan Catalogue* Part A (British Isles) 1984 which describes the surviving plans in the ownership of Chas E Goad Ltd (18a Salisbury Square, Old Hatfield, Hertfordshire AL5 5BE).

Personal Records

PRIVATE PAPERS

Sometimes useful business records are in the ownership of private individuals who were owners, important shareholders, partners, directors or senior managers. If deceased, their papers may have passed to their descendants. If the individual was an important shareholder these records might include annual reports, shareholders' circulars and copies of the chairman's statement to annual general meetings; if a partner, they might include partnership deeds or even partnership accounts; if a director, they might be board minutes, papers submitted to the board, files of correspondence, photographs, brochures and diaries. Directors of large companies frequently held several non-executive directorships and, if relevant papers have not survived amongst their private papers, they might be hold in the archives of the company with which the director was most closely connected. In identifying the different directorships held by an individual the *Directory of Directors*, first published in 1880, is helpful.

The National Register of Archives maintains a computer-based Personal Names Index relating to the location of personal papers, but it includes only papers of those people listed in the *Dictionary of National Biography*, *Who Was Who* and other biographical reference books, and which have been reported to the Register.

WILLS

Wills and letters of administration (most frequently issued in connection with the administration of intestate estates) provide a certain amount of information about businessmen and are the most useful when there is a shortage of information from other sources. Wills provide details of occupation, address, name and relationship of beneficiaries, particulars of estate, and names of executors and witnesses (often business associates). They assume a greater importance if supported by an inventory of the deceased's property, listing and valuing the composition of the estate. These were obligatory before 1782 but unfortunately they do not survive in large numbers and they relate mostly to the sixteenth, seventeenth and eighteenth centuries, although for much longer in Scotland. The usefulness of wills is also tempered by the fact that property recorded in a will might not necessarily represent the whole property accumulated during the deceased's lifetime. Even before the introduction of estate duty and successor taxes, property was frequently transferred prior to death.

Before 1858 wills were a matter for ecclesiastical authority, and were proved in various, most frequently local, ecclesiastical courts. This arrangement was terminated by the Court of Probate Act 1857 which established the Principal Probate Registry in London, supported by a number of subordinated district registries. These registries inherited the Church's records of wills and, latterly, these have passed into the custody of local record offices. The Public Record Office has the records of the Prerogative Court of Canterbury and the Borthwick Institute of Historical Research in York has the records of the Prerogative Court of York.

Records of post-1857 wills proved in England and Wales are located at Somerset House, The Strand, London WC2R 1LP. Knowledge of the year of death of the testator is useful as indexes are arranged alphabetically by year. Scottish wills proved prior to 1823 are in the Scottish Record Office (SRO). Since then they have been proved locally and are with the relevant Sheriff Clerk or have been deposited in the SRO. The National Library of Wales houses Welsh wills proved prior to 1858, while subsequent wills are at Somerset House. From 1796 until 1903 abstracts of all wills in England and Wales had to be deposited with the Estate (or Stamp) Duty Office for tax purposes. Registers of abstracts survive and are available in the Public Record Office in class IR26. Indexes are in class IR27. They record date of probate, all beneficiaries, and details and value of property. However, a 125-years closure period is enforced.

Useful further reading on wills includes A J Camp *Wills and Their Whereabouts* (1974), J S W Gibson *Wills and Where to Find Them* (Chichester, 1974) and J S W Gibson *A Simplified Guide to Probate Jurisdiction* (1982). The Public Record Office produces a leaflet, 'Probate Records', which gives details of its holdings of wills and inventories.

CENSUS RECORDS

Another source which sheds some light on the businessman as an individual is national census records. The earliest census was held in 1801 and censuses have been held virtually every ten years since then. However, the earliest censuses were only concerned with population totals and it was not until 1841 that personal details of individuals were recorded. However, these details were limited in scope, giving little more than date and place of birth, occupation, and relationship of members of a household. Where employees live on the premises they are named and their grade is given. This is especially so of shop workers. Census records are only available for general public inspection when they are 100 years old. Microfilm copies are available for consultation in the Public Record Office's Census Room (Portugal St, London WC2), and many local record offices and local history libraries have acquired copies covering their localities. J S W Gibson *Census Returns 1841–1881 On Microfilm. A Directory of Local Holdings* (4th edition, 1983) is a useful guide to what is available locally. The usefulness of censuses is tempered by the need for a precise address, which is most essential in searching for details of town residents, but trade directories can often help in this. The PRO publishes a leaflet on the use of census records, *Censuses of Population 1801–1881*.

INTERVIEWS

Interviews with directors, partners and managers – and sometimes their descendants – can provide useful information and, at the least, help to compensate for lack of records. They yield information and opinions on motives, personalities, internal politics and work processes, a paper record of which is often not made at the time.

Paul Thompson *The Voice of the Past. Oral History* (Oxford, 1978) covers a wide range of subjects concerned with oral history and not least gives useful practical advice on interview technique.

Visual Sources

INDUSTRIAL ARCHAEOLOGY

One source of information frequently overlooked is the nature of the building, and its location, from which the business operated. The inner areas of Britain's cities, where historically business activity has been concentrated, have been ravaged by post–1945 developments but much still survives. A visit to the business's address can at once provide an impression of scale of operations, both absolute and relative to adjacent buildings; proximity to transport facilities and markets; proximity to the city/town centre and managers' and workers' housing; and date(s) of building(s) and of extensions to them. The rapidly growing number of technology, transport and industrial museums (not least the Science Museum) have exhibits (most not displayed due to lack of space) and other information concerning machinery, other capital equipment and production processes which would have taken place in these buildings.

Many local industrial archaeology societies exist which have completed excellent field work, the results of which have often been published in their newsletters or journals. The Newsletter of the Greater London Industrial Archaeology Society and the Journal of the Norfolk Industrial Archaeology Society are worthy of special mention. An umbrella organisation is the Association for Industrial Archaeology.

Techniques of industrial archaeology are covered in Kenneth Hudson *Industrial Archaeology. An Introduction* (London, 1963) and R A Buchanan *Industrial Archaeology in Britain* (Harmondsworth, revised edition 1985). *Industrial Archaeology* (first published in 1964 as the *Journal of Industrial Archaeology*) and *Industrial Archaeology Review* (first published in 1976) are useful periodicals.

Other sources of literature concerning buildings and factories include periodicals such as *The Builder* (published from 1843), which often carried reports, and sometimes illustrations, of large building projects. It is indexed. Other periodicals include *The Architects' Journal* and *Building News*.

PHOTOGRAPHS, PRINTS AND DRAWINGS

Photographs, and sometimes prints and drawings of buildings, machinery, goods produced, work processes and employees form a useful source of information and a substitute or supplement to industrial archaeology field work.

Museums, record offices and local history libraries have useful photograph collections but so do private individuals, businesses and professional photographers. Every town probably had at least one professional photographer from the early twentieth century and his/her photographs of local scenes and personalities are invaluable. Sometimes they have been deposited in local record offices or remain with the business if it survives. A useful guide to collections of photographs, in both public and private hands, is John Wall *Directory of British Photographic Collections* (London, 1977). It is comprehensive and well indexed but rather oddly arranged. Of more general importance is John West *Town Records* (Chichester, 1983) which provides a list of photograph collections, arranged by town and covering the years 1840 to the present.

The National Monuments Record, based in London, The Royal Commission on Ancient and Historical Monuments in Wales (in Aberystwyth) and the National Monuments Record of Scotland (in Edinburgh) have valuable collections of photographs, plans, drawings and fieldwork reports. While earlier photographic material is held, these photograph collections trace their origins to a photographic record of buildings threatened by war, instigated in 1941.

There are also a number of picture libraries which operate on a commercial basis, charging users a fee. The best known is the Radio Times Hulton Picture Library in London.

EPHEMERA

This includes a vast range of materials – from bus tickets to greeting cards, from letter heads to bottle labels. Much of this is discarded and destroyed as a matter of routine. Nevertheless, the ephemera created by a business give an interesting insight into its history – especially its advertising and promotion – and also provide illustrative material. Most collections are in private hands, amassed by enthusiasts. Many collectors belong to the Ephemera Society which publishes a newsletter *The Ephemerist* (first published 1975) and occasional publications such as *Bill of Fare. An Exhibition of the Ephemera of Food and Drink* (London, 1984). The John Johnson Collection of Printed Ephemera, held in the Bodleian Library, Oxford, is one of the largest collections in public hands and its massive size and diversity is indicated in *The John Johnson Collection. Catalogue of an Exhibition* (Oxford, 1971) which is available from the Bodleian Library. Guildhall Library has an extensive collection of eighteenth and nineteenth-century trade cards and bill heads. The British Library also has a large collection. Sir Ambrose Heal wrote extensively about trades-men's cards, shop signs and other items of ephemera. His books include *London Tradesmen's Cards of the Eighteenth Century* (London, 1925), which contains illustrations of over 100 cards, and *The Sign Boards of Old London Shops* (London, 1957).

Bibliography

The bibliography includes all works quoted in the text

N W Alcock *Old Title Deeds. A Guide for Local and Family Historians* (Chichester, 1986)

John Armstrong & Stephanie Jones *Business Documents. Their Origins, Sources and Uses to the Historian* (London, 1987)

William Bailey *List of Bankrupts*

G S Bain & G B Woolven *A Bibliography of British Industrial Relations* (Cambridge, 1979)

The Bankers' Almanac and Year Book (first published 1845)

The Bankrupts' Register (annually 1833–48)

Joyce M Bellamy & John Saville (eds) *The Dictionary of Labour Biography* (London, 1972–)

J M Bellamy *Yorkshire Business Histories. A Bibliography* (Bradford, 1970)

John Benson, Robert G Neville & Charles H Thompson *Bibliography of the British Coal Industry. Secondary Literature, Parliamentary and Department Papers, Mineral Maps and Plans, and a Guide to Sources* (Oxford, 1981)

Maurice Beresford 'Building History from Fire Insurance Records', *Urban History Year Book* (1976)

Valerie Bloomfield *Resources for Canadian Studies in Britain with some References to Europe* (British Association for Canadian Studies, London, 2nd ed, 1983)

Bodleian Library *The John Johnson Collection. Catalogue of an Exhibition* (Oxford, 1971)

Britain's Privately Owned Companies. Second 2000 (first published 1984)

Britain's Top 2000 Private Companies (first published 1984)

British Association of Industrial Editors *British House Journals* (London, 1956)

British Union Catalogue of Periodicals. A Record of the Periodicals of the World from the Seventeenth Century to the Present Day in British Libraries (4 vols, London, 1955–58, and subsequent supplements)

R A Buchanan *Industrial Archaeology in Britain* (Harmondsworth, rev ed, 1985)

The Builder (first published 1843)

Burdett's Official Intelligence (annually 1882–98). Continued as *Stock Exchange Official Intelligence* (annually 1899–1933) and *Stock Exchange Year Book* (annually from 1934)

Business Archives (first published 1958)

Business Archives Council (John Armstrong ed) *Directory of Corporate Archives* (1985, revised ed,1987)

Business History (first published 1958)

A J Camp *Wills and Their Whereabouts* (London, 1974)

S D Chapman 'Business History from Insurance Policy Registers' *Business Archives* 32 (June 1970)

S D Chapman *The Devon Cloth Industry in the Eighteenth Century. Sun Fire Office Inventories of Merchants' and Manufacturers' Property* (Devon and Cornwall Records Society, New Series, 23, 1978)

Chemical Manufacturers' Directory (first published 1867)

H A L Cockerell & Edwin Green *The British Insurance Business 1547–1970* (London, 1976)

Construction History (first published 1985)

C R H Cooper 'The Archives of the City of London Livery Companies and Related Organisations' *Archives* 72 (Oct 1984)

J Cornwall *How to Read Old Title Deeds* (London, 1964)

The Course of Exchange (first published 1697)

Nicholas Cox 'The Records of the Register General of Shipping and Seamen' *Maritime History* 11 (1972)

Current British Directories (first published 1953)

A A Dibben *Title Deeds* (Historical Association, London, 1968)

Directory of British Associations (first published 1965)

Directory of Directors (first published 1880)

James Douglas *Scottish Banknotes* (London, 1975)

The Dublin Gazette (first published 1705; known as *Iris Oifigiul* since 1922)

The Economist (first published 1843)

The Edinburgh Gazette (first published 1680)

J A Edwards *Historical Farm Records: A Summary Guide to Manuscripts and other Material in the University Library Collected by the Institute of Agricultural History and Museum of English Rural Life* (Reading, 1973)

J A Edwards 'Publishers' Archives at Reading University' *Business Archives* 45 (Nov 1979)

J R Edwards *Company Legislation and Changing Patterns of Disclosure in British Company Accounts 1900–1940* (The Institute of Chartered Accountants in England and Wales, London, 1981)

George Elwick *A Complete Register of All Bankrupts* (London, 1843)

F G Emmison *Guide to the Essex Record Office* (Chelmsford, 1969)

Ephemera Society *Bill of Fare. An Exhibition of the Ephemera of Food and Drink* (London, 1984)

The Ephemerist (first published 1975)

Fairplay's Annual Summary of British Shipping Finance (published 1925–51)

Joan P S Ferguson *Dictionary of Scottish Newspapers* (Edinburgh, 1984)

P Ford & G Ford *A Breviate of Parliamentary Papers. The Foundation of the Welfare State* (Oxford, 1957)

P Ford & G Ford *A Breviate of Parliamentary Papers 1917–1939* (Oxford, 1951)

P Ford & G Ford *A Breviate of Parliamentary Papers 1940–1954* (Oxford, 1961)

P Ford & G Ford *A Guide to Parliamentary Papers* (3rd ed, Shannon, Ireland, 1972)

Janet Foster & Julia Sheppard *British Archives. A Guide to Archive Resources in the United Kingdom* (London, 1982, revised 1984, 2nd ed in preparation 1987)

J S W Gibson *Census Records 1841–1881 on Microfilm. A Directory of Local Holdings* (Federation of Family History Societies, Plymouth, 4th ed, 1982)

J S W Gibson *Simplified Guide to Probate Jurisdiction* (Federation of Family History Societies, Plymouth, 3rd ed, 1985)

J S W Gibson *Wills and Where to Find Them* (Chichester, 1974)

Chas E Goad Ltd *Goad Fire Insurance Plan Catalogue. The British Isles* (Old Hatfield, 1984)

Honor Godfrey 'British Business Archives – The Archives of J Sainsbury Limited' *Business Archives* 44 (Nov 1978)

Francis Goodall *Bibliography of British Business Histories* (Aldershot, 1987)

C W F Goss *The London Directories 1677–1855* (London, 1932)

G L Grant *The Standard Catalogue of Provincial Banks and Banks Notes* (London, 1977)

Edwin Green 'Bank Archives for Historians. The Case of Midland Bank's Archives' *Business Archives* 49 (Nov 1983)

C R Hall *A Guide to the Lloyd's Marine Collection at Guildhall Library* (Guildhall Library, London, 1985)

H Harding *Patent Office Centenary. A Story of 100 Years in the Life and Work of the Patent Office* (London, 1953, reprinted 1975)

Susan M Hare 'The Records of the Goldsmiths' Company' *Archives* 72 (Oct 1984)

J B Harley *The Historian's Guide to Ordnance Survey Maps* (Standing Conference for Local History, London, 1964)

Sir Ambrose Heal *London Tradesmen's Cards of the XVIII Century. An Account of their Origin and Use* (London, 1925)

Sir Ambrose Heal *The Signboards of Old London Shops; A Review of... Shop Signs Employed by London Tradesmen during the XVIIth and XVIIIth centuries* (London, 1947)

F G Hilton Price *A Handbook of London Bankers* (London, 1890–91)

Kenneth Hudson *Industrial Archaeology. An Introduction* (London, 1963)

Patricia Hudson *The West Riding Wool Textile Industry. A Catalogue of Business Records from the Sixteenth to the Twentieth Century* (Edington, 1975)

Industrial Archaeology (first published 1964)

Industrial Archaeology Review (first published 1976)

The Insurance Directory and Year Book (first published 1842)

The Investors' Chronicle (first published 1860)

93

The Investors' Guardian and Limited Liability Review subsequently *Investors' Guardian* (first published 1863)

D T Jenkins *Indexes of the Fire Insurance Policies of the Sun Fire Office and the Royal Exchange Assurance 1775–1787* (York, 1986)

David J Jeremy (ed) *Dictionary of Business Biography. A Biographical Dictionary of Business Leaders Active in Britain in the Period 1860–1980* (5 vols, London, 1984–86)

L C Johnson 'British Transport Commission Archive: Work Since 1953' *Journal of Transport History* 5 (May 1962)

L C Johnson 'Historical Records of the British Transport Commission' *Journal of Transport History* 1 (Nov 1953)

Charles A Jones *Britain and the Dominions. A Guide to Business and Related Records in the United Kingdom Concerning Australia, Canada, New Zealand and South Africa* (Boston, Mass, 1978)

Edgar Jones *Accountancy and the British Economy 1840–1980. The Evolution of Ernst & Whinney* (London, 1981)

Edgar Jones *Industrial Architecture in Britain 1750–1939* (London, 1985)

Michael E Keen *A Bibliography of the Trade Directories . . . in the National Art Library* (Victoria & Albert Museum, London, 1979)

A M Kennett *Archives and Records of the City of Chester* (Chester, 1985)

Key British Enterprises. The Top 20,000 British Companies (first published 1961)

Kompass Directory (first published 1962)

Joan Lane *Register of Business Records of Coventry and Related Areas* (Coventry, 1977)

Leeds Archives Dept *Sources of Business and Industrial History in Leeds Archives Department* (Leeds, 1977)

Sarah Levitt 'The Uses of Registered Design Samples in the Public Record Office, Kew, for the Study of Nineteenth Century Clothing Manufacturers' *Business Archives* 50 (Nov 1984)

David Linton & Ray Boston (eds) *The Newspaper Press in Britain: An Annotated Bibliography* (London, 1987)

M Livingstone *Guide to the Public Records of Scotland* (Edinburgh, 1905)

The London Gazette (since 1665; published as *The Oxford Gazette* 1665–1700)

Jane Lowe *A Guide to Sources in the History of the Cycle and Motor Industries in Coventry 1880–1939* (Coventry, 1982)

Ian MacDougall *A Catalogue of Some Labour Records in Scotland and some Scottish Records Outside Scotland* (Edinburgh, 1978)

Angela Mace *The Royal Institute of British Architects. A Guide to its Archives and History* (London, 1986)

Macmillan's Unquoted Companies (published from 1985)

Phyllis Mander-Jones *Manuscripts in the British Isles Relating to Australia, New Zealand and the Pacific* (Canberra, Australia, 1972)

Sheila Marriner 'English Bankruptcy Records and Statistics Before 1850' *Economic History Review* 33 (Aug 1980)

Sheila Marriner 'Company Financial Statements as Source Material for Business Historians' *Business History* 22 (Jul 1980)

Arthur Marsh & Victoria Ryan *Historical Directory of Trade Unions* (Aldershot, 1980–)

Peter Mathias & A W H Pearsall *Shipping. A Survey of Historical Records* (Newton Abbot, 1971)

Noel Matthews & M Doreen Wainwright *A Guide to Manuscripts and Documents in the British Isles Relating to Africa* (Oxford, 1971)

Noel Matthews & M D Wainwright *A Guide to Manuscripts and Documents in the British Isles Relating to the Far East* (Oxford, 1977)

Noel Matthews & M D Wainwright *A Guide to Manuscripts and Documents in the British Isles Relating to the Middle East and North Africa* (Oxford, 1980)

H Campbell McMurray 'The Records of the Shipbuilders' and Repairers' National Association' *Business Archives* 45 (Nov 1979)

Patricia Millard (ed) *Trade Associations and Professional Bodies of the United Kingdom* (1st ed 1962, 7th ed 1985)

R C Mitchie *Money, Mania and Markets. Investment, Company Formation and the Stock Exchange in Nineteenth Century Scotland* (Edinburgh, 1981)

Modern Records Centre *Trade Union and Related Records* (Coventry, 3rd ed, 1983)

E Victor Morgan & W A Thomas *The Stock Exchange. Its History and Function* (London, 1962)

Michael Moss 'Forgotten Ledgers, Law and the Business Historian; Gleanings from the Adam Smith Business Collection' *Archives* 16 (Oct 1984)

Michael Moss & J R Hume 'Business Failure in Scotland 1839–1913: A Research Note' *Business History* 25 (Mar 1983)

National Maritime Museum *Guide to the Manuscripts of the National Maritime Museum. Public Records, Business Records and Artificial Collections*, vol 2 (London, 1980)

T R Nevett *Advertising in Britain. A History* (London, 1982)

Newspaper Press Directory (published from 1849)

Jane E Norton *Guide to National and Provincial Directories of England and Wales, Excluding London, Published Before 1856* (Royal Historical Society, London, 1950)

John Orbell 'A Note on Series J 90 in the Public Record Office' *Business Archives* 49 (Nov 1983)

George Ottley *A Bibliography of British Railway History* (London, 2nd ed, 1983)

Patent Office *A Century of Trade Marks* (London, 1976)

Peter L Payne *The Early Scottish Limited Companies 1856–1895* (Edinburgh, 1980)

Peter Payne *Studies in Scottish Business History* (London, 1967)

Perry's Gazette (first published in 1828 as *Perry's Bankrupt & Insolvent Weekly Gazette* and known as *Perry's Bankrupt Weekly Gazette* 1862–1881)

Gordon Phillips 'The Archives of *The Times*' *Business Archives* 41 (Jan 1976)

Lorna Poole 'British Business Archives – The John Lewis Partnership' *Business Archives* 37 (Dec 1972)

Post Office Directory of London (W Kelly & Co, London, first published 1841)

L S Pressnell & John Orbell *Guide to the Historical Records of British Banking* (Aldershot, 1985)

Public Record Office *Guide to the Contents of the Public Record Office*, 3 vols (HMSO, 1963–68)

Public Record Office *Maps and Plans in the Public Record Office. The British Isles* (HMSO, 1967)

Public Record Office *Public Records Relating to Commerce and Industry* (Public Record Office, 1985)

Public Record Office of Northern Ireland *The Ulster Textile Industry. A Catalogue of Business Records in PRONI relating principally to the Linen Industry in Ulster* (Belfast, 1978)

Railway Year Book (published 1898–1932)

John W Raimo *A Guide to Manuscripts Relating to America in Great Britain and Ireland* (London, 1979)

Gordon Read 'The Bryson Collection of Business Archives and Ephemera' *Business Archives* 47 (Nov 1981)

The Red Book of Commerce or Who's Who in Business (published 1906–39)

Lesley Richmond & Bridget Stockford *Company Archives. A Survey of the Records of the First Registered Companies in England and Wales* (Aldershot, 1986)

L A Ritchie *Modern British Shipbuilding. A Guide to Historical Records* (London, 1980)

E M Rodger *The Large Scale County Maps of the British Isles 1596–1850. A Union List* (Oxford, 1972)

Frank Rodgers *A Guide to British Government Publications* (New York, 1980)

D J Rowe *Northern Business History. A Bibliography* (London, 1979)

Gwyn Rowley 'British Fire Insurance Plans. The Goad Productions c1885–c1970' *Archives* 74 (Oct 1985)

Royal Commission on Historical Manuscripts *Accessions to Repositories and Reports Added to the National Register of Archives* (HMSO, from 1954)

Royal Commission on Historical Manuscripts *Architectural History and the Fine and Applied Arts: Sources in the National Register of Archives* (HMSO, annually 1969–74)

Royal Commission on Historical Manuscripts *Record Repositories in Great Britain. A Geographical Directory* (HMSO, 8th ed, 1987)

Royal Commission on Historical Manuscripts *Sources of Business History in the National Register of Archives* (HMSO, annually 1964–72)

Royal Commission on Historical Manuscripts *Sources for the*

History in the National Register of Archives (HMSO, annually 1964–72)

Royal Commission on Historical Manuscripts *Sources for the History of British Business and Industry 1760–1914* (forthcoming series)

Scottish Industrial History (first published 1976)

Scottish Record Office *Annual Report of the Keeper of the Records of Scotland* (annually)

Scottish Record Office *Descriptive List of Plans in the Scottish Record Office* 3 vols (HMSO, 1966–74)

R Sharpe France *Guide to the Lancashire Record Office* (Preston, 1962, revised ed 1985)

Sheffield City Libraries *Patent Holdings in British Public Libraries* (Sheffield, 1973)

The Shorter Aslib Directory of Information Sources in the United Kingdom (first published 1986)

Anthony Slaven & Sydney Checkland *Dictionary of Scottish Business Biography 1860–1960* 2 vols (Aberdeen, 1986–87)

Judy Slinn *A History of Freshfields* (London, 1984)

William Smith & Co *A List of Bankrupts with their Dividends, Certificates, etc, from Jan 1 1780 to Jun 24 1806 Inclusive* (London, 1806)

Society of Genealogists *The Apprentices of Great Britain 1710–1762* (33 vols, typescript, Society of Genealogists, London, 1928–36)

Society of Genealogists *The Apprentices of Great Britain 1763–1774* (7 vols, typescript, Society of Genealogists, London, 1937–41)

Society of Genealogists *Index to the Names of the Masters* (7 vols, typescript, Society of Genealogists, London, 1931–42)

The Statist (first published 1878)

The Stock Exchange Register of Defunct Companies (last published 1980)

Stock Exchange Year Book (first published 1876). Known as *Stock Exchange Official Year Book* from 1934. (see *Burdett's Official Intelligence*)

Richard Storey 'Bibliography of Histories of Employers' and

Trade Organisations' *Broadsheet* 4 (Business Archives Council, London, 1979)

Richard Storey & Susan Edwards *Supplement to the Guide to the Modern Records Centre* (Coventry, 1981)

Richard Storey & Alistair Tough *Consolidated Guide to the Modern Records Centre* (Coventry, 1986)

Richard Storey & Janet Druker *Guide to the Modern Records Centre* (Coventry, 1977)

Brenda Swann & Maureen Turnbull *Records of Interest to Social Scientists 1919 to 1930* (Public Record Office Handbook No 14, HMSO, 1971)

Lenore Symons 'Archives and Records of the Institution of Electrical Engineers' *Archives* 16 (Apr 1983)

W A Thomas *The Provincial Stock Exchanges. Their History and Function* (London, 1973)

W A Thomas *Stock Exchanges of Ireland* (Liverpool, 1986)

Paul Thompson *The Voice of the Past. Oral History* (Oxford, 1978)

Alison Turton 'British Business Archives – The Archives of the House of Fraser Ltd' *Business Archives* 46 (Nov 1980)

M D Wainwright & Noel Matthews *A Guide to Western Manuscripts and Documents in the British Isles Relating to South and South East Asia* (Oxford, 1965)

John Wall *Directory of British Photographic Collections* (London, 1977)

Peter Walne (ed) *A Guide to Manuscript Sources for the History of Latin America and the Caribbean in the British Isles* (Oxford, 1973)

D B Wardle 'Sources for the History of Railways in the Public Record Office' *Journal of Transport History* 2 (Nov 1956)

Waterloo Directory of Victorian Periodicals 1824–1900 (University of Waterloo & Wilfred Laurier University Press, Waterloo, Canada, 1976)

Ian Watt *A Directory of UK Map Collections* (Map Curators' Group Publication, 1985)

Christopher T Watts & Michael J Watts 'Company Records as a Source for the Family Historian' *Genealogists' Magazine* 21 (Jun 1983)

John West *Town Records* (Chichester, 1983)

Oliver M Westall *The Historian and the Business of Insurance* (Manchester, 1984)

Who Owns Whom. United Kingdom and Republic of Ireland (published from 1958)

Michael Wilcox *The Confederation of British Industry Predecessor Archives* (Coventry, 1984)

Willing's Press Guide (published from 1874)

Brian Winship 'Patents as an Historical Source' *Industrial Archaeology* 16 (1981)

Bennet Woodcroft *Alphabetical Index of Patenters of Inventions* (London, 1854, republished 1969)

Addresses

The addresses of all record offices, libraries, museums, societies and other organisations quoted in the text are given below.

Aberdeen University Library
Manuscripts and Archives Section
King's College Library
Aberdeen AB9 2UB
tel: 0224 40241

Association for Industrial Archaeology
The Wharfage
Ironbridge
Telford
Shropshire TF8 7AW

Birmingham Reference Library
Central Libraries
Chamberlain Square
Birmingham
West Midlands B3 3HQ
tel: 021 235 4219

Bodleian Library
Oxford University
Oxford OX1 3BG
tel: 0865 244675

Borthwick Institute of Historical Research
University of York
St Anthony's Hall
Peasholme Green
York YO1 2PW
tel: 0904 59861

Bristol University Library
Tyndall Avenue
Bristol
Avon BS8 1TJ
tel: 0272 24161

British Architectural Library
Royal Institute of British Architects (RIBA)
66 Portland Place
London W1N 4AD
tel: 01 580 5533

British Association of Industrial Editors
3 Lock's Yard
High Street
Sevenoaks
Kent TN13 1LT
tel: 0732 459331

British Library
Great Russell St
London WC1B 3DG
tel: 01 636 1544

British Library Newspaper Library
Colindale Avenue
London NW9 5HE
tel: 01 200 5515

British Records Association
Master's Court
The Charterhouse
Charterhouse Square
London EC1M 6AU
tel: 01 253 0436

Business Archives Council (BAC)
185 Tower Bridge Road
London SE1 2UF
tel: 01 407 6110

Business Archives Council of Scotland (BACS)
Glasgow University Archives
The University
Glasgow G12 8QQ
tel: 041 339 8855

Business History Unit
London School of Economics
Lionel Robbins Building
10 Portugal Street
London WC2A 2HD
tel: 01 405 7686

Cambridge University Library
Cambridge University
West Road
Cambridge CB3 9DR
tel: 0223 61441

Chester City Record Office
Town Hall
Chester
Cheshire CH1 2HJ
tel: 0244 40144

City Business Library
55 Basinghall Street
London EC2
tel: 01 638 8215

Construction History Society
c/o The Chartered Institute of Building
Englemere
King's Ride
Ascot
Berkshire

Corporation of London Record Office
Guildhall
London EC2P 2EJ

Coventry City Record Office
Room 220
Broadgate House
Broadgate
Coventry
West Midlands CV1 1NG
tel: 0203 25555

Ephemera Society
12 Fitzroy Square
London W1P 5HQ
tel: 01 387 7723

Essex Record Office
County Hall
Chelmsford
Essex CM1 1LX
tel: 0245 267222

Glasgow University Archives
The University
Glasgow G12 8QQ
tel: 041 339 8855

Chas E Goad Ltd
18a Salisbury Square
Old Hatfield
Hertfordshire AL9 5BE

Greater London Industrial Archaeology Society
Hon Secretary
30 Gaveston Drive
Berkhampstead
Hertfordshire HP4 1JF

Greater London Record Office
40 Northampton Road
London EC1R 0HB
tel: 01 633 6851

Guildhall Library
Aldermanbury
London EC2P 2EJ
tel: 01 606 3030

History of Advertising Trust
Unit 2.02
Butler's Wharf Business Centre
45 Curlew Street
London SE1 2ND
tel: 01 403 0756

Hull City Record Office
79 Lowgate
Kingston upon Hull
Humberside HU1 2AA
tel: 0482 222015/6

Institute of Agricultural History and Museum of
English Rural Life
University of Reading
Whiteknights
Reading
Berkshire RG6 2AG
tel: 0734 875123

Institute of Historical Research
University of London
Senate House
London WC1E 7HU
tel: 01 636 0272

Institute of Electrical Engineers
Archives Dept
Savoy Place
London WC2R 0BL
tel: 01 240 1871

John Rylands University Library of Manchester
University of Manchester
Deansgate
Manchester M3 3EH
tel: 061 834 5343

Lancashire Record Office
Bow Lane
Preston
Lancashire PR1 8ND
tel: 0772 54868

Leeds District Archives
Chapeltown Road
Sheepscar
Leeds
West Yorkshire LS7 3AP

Memorial University of Newfoundland
St John's
Newfoundland
Canada

Modern Records Centre
University of Warwick Library
Coventry
West Midlands CV4 7AL
tel: 0203 523523

National Library of Wales
Aberystwyth
Dyfed SY23 3BU
tel: 0970 3816

National Maritime Museum
Romney Road
Greenwich
London SE10 9NF
tel: 01 858 4422

National Monuments Record
Fortress House
23 Savile Row
London W1X 1AB
tel: 01 734 6010

National Monuments Record of Scotland
54 Melville Street
Edinburgh EH3 7HF
tel: 031 225 5994

National Register of Archives (NRA)
Quality House
Quality Court
Chancery Lane
London WC2A 1HP
tel: 01 242 1198

National Register of Archives (Scotland) (NRAS)
HM General Register House
P O Box 36
Edinburgh EH1 3YY
tel: 031 556 6585

Public Record Office (PRO)
Ruskin Avenue
Kew
Richmond
Surrey TW9 4DU
tel: 01 876 3444

and

Chancery Lane
London WC2 1AH
tel: 01 405 0741

Public Record Office (PRO)
Census Search Room
Land Registry Building
Portugal Street
London WC2A 3HP
tel: 01 405 3488

Public Record Office of Northern Ireland (PRONI)
66 Balmoral Avenue
Belfast BT9 6NY
tel: 0232 661621

Radio Times Hulton Picture Library
35 Marylebone High Street
London W1
tel: 01 580 5577

Reading University
Dept of Archives and Manuscripts
Whiteknights
Reading
Berkshire RG6 2AE
tel: 0734 875123

Register of Companies for England and Wales
Companies Registration Office
Crown Way
Maindy
Cardiff CF4 3U2
tel: 0222 388588

and

London Search Room
Companies House
City Road
London EC1Y 1BB
tel: 01 253 9393

Register of Companies for Northern Ireland
IDB House
64 Chichester Street
Belfast BT1 4JX
tel: 0232 234488

Register of Companies for Scotland
102 George Street
Edinburgh EH2 3DJ
tel: 031 225 5774

Royal Air Force Museum
Dept of Aviation Records
Aerodrome Road
Hendon
London NW9 5LL
tel: 01 205 2266

Royal Commission on Ancient and Historical
Monuments in Wales
Edleston House
Queen's Road
Aberystwyth
Dyfed SY23 2HP
tel: 0970 4381/2

Royal Commission on Historical Manuscripts (HMC)
Quality House
Quality Court
Chancery Lane
London WC2A 1HP
tel: 01 242 1198

Science Museum
Exhibition Road
London SW7 5NH
tel: 01 589 3456

Science Reference Library
25 Southampton Buildings
Chancery Lane
London WC2A 1AW
tel: 01 405 8721

Scottish Record Office (SRO)
HM General Register House
Princes Street
Edinburgh EH1 3YY
tel: 031 556 6585

Telecom Technology Showcase
Baynard House
135 Queen Victoria Street
London EC4V 4AT

Tyne & Wear Archive Service
Blandford House
West Blandford Street
Newcastle upon Tyne
Tyne & Wear NE1 4JA
tel: 0632 326789

University College
University of London
Gower Street
London WC1E 6BT
tel: 01 387 7050

Victoria & Albert Museum
Cromwell Road
South Kensington
London SW7 2RL
tel: 01 589 6371

Index